HEAL YOUR LIFE

Nourish Your Body and Soul

Manal Shabani

Heal Your Life: Nourish Your Body and Soul

ISBN: 9781079276381

Published by:
10-10-10 Publishing
455 Apple Creek Boulevard
Suite 200
Markham, Ontario
L3R 9X7

Table of Contents

About the Book and Author

I went through hundreds upon thousands of studies and articles (which I have been studying in the last 20 years) about the effect of healthy food, meditation, and lifestyle for healing yourself and your family. With the information in this book, I managed to heal my life and my family's life too, from deadly but preventable diseases.

I used my psychology, family counselling, and nutrition therapy background, plus my work and personal experience, to put this book together and in your hands.

My aim in this book is to save millions of people around the world, who struggle to cure themselves from the instability of personal, financial, emotional, and preventable medical conditions.

When you believe in yourself and accept making the positive changes, you will manage to heal yourself, be stronger, and be capable of making the impossible, easy and possible.

You will find evidence and tools to live happier, healthier, and longer, I am sure you will be able to make your life 100% better.

I'm not offering you medication, or expensive equipment, but I am providing you with information and education that is worth more than diamonds, and it will change your life to the best it can be and you will be the person you always wish to be.

You need to start taking control of your body and soul, and believing in yourself. Trust your children's abilities as soon as they see the light. Your child, just as you were, is a result of a successful egg that managed to pick up the strongest and best sperm from millions of other sperm. Children are far smarter than we know, and they are winners, just as you are. You are smart and able, but you might be controlled by the rules that your parents and school taught you, believing that they were the best for you. Believing in yourself and your children's abilities can be the huge transferable improvement in your life.

Believing in our abilities, and our children's, is the key for the biggest achievement and success. If all of us let our love and interests motivate us, we will all live healthier and happier lives, and in peace.

I provide you, in this book, with the real healthy food, but what is more important is healing yourself, using the best loneliness prescription to nourish your body and soul. Live in peace by allowing your parasympathetic nervous system and its relaxation responses to take the control, instead of the fight or flight mode, which puts your life upside down with toxic relationships and wrong choices.

Allow your children to live in an indefinite, healthy, successful, and happy life. Stay strong and happy on your feet to the last day of your life, by preventing all the preventable diseases.

This book is written in a way that is easy to understand, for you, the children, the grand-children, and the grandparents.

Acknowledgements

My love for my two daughters and husband is what really motivated me to do the intensive research in the last twenty years, to learn about the very healthy life, and to build a happy family. A big thank you to my husband and children (Melissa and Melinda). They motivated me to heal my family and myself.

I would also like to thank Dr. Hanna Kazkaz and Dr. Vikkhullar, who respect and trust my way of listening to my body, and for helping me with the incurable EDS. They both supported me, and they brought to my attention the need of pacing. Listening to our bodies is the best way to keep our parasympathetic nervous system, or what is called the relaxation response, in a good state to stay free from symptoms, which only pull us down and do not allow us to enjoy life.

On the 9th of December, 2018, I had the wakeup call from Raymond. He sent me back in my memory, to 1991, when Dr Jihad Elkhatib, a group dynamic and family counselor lecturer at Jordan University, was saying to us, loudly, “What are you waiting for? There is nothing you can’t do, but you’re too lazy to move. Live now, and live today like there is no tomorrow, and enjoy it. Do not look back or worry about the future. The future will be perfect only if we learn how to change the impossible to the possible, via the huge energy that is born within us, and enjoy life in the present."

Foreword

Do you believe that you can live a healthier, happier and more successful life, just by connecting with yourself, accepting yourself as you are, and then connecting with a strong, positive network?

In *Heal Your Life,* author Manal Shabani shows you, step by step, how to heal your soul and body by nourishing them not only with the best food and drink, but also by caring for yourself by using valuable techniques such as breathing and meditation, in each stage of your life. You will become aware of the difference between the hidden, toxic and strongly masked foods and drinks that jeopardize your health, and learn about healthier real foods and drinks that will boost your energy and brain function, and make you stronger.

I am very sure if you read her book and learn from the rich information provided, you will not only eat and drink healthier, but you will also enjoy better relationships, you will be happier, and you will see your dreams come true. Manal talks about the need to detoxify yourself inside and out, physically, mentally and emotionally, to help you reach any goal that you set for yourself.

I found *Heal Your Life* to be rich with useful information about living your best life, and I have no doubt that you will agree with me!

Raymond Aaron
New York Times Bestselling Author

Chapter 1

The Loneliness and Your Health

We could wonder what the most important part of our health is. Is it eating a balanced, vegetarian diet, limiting animal products? Is it the perfect lifestyle via sleeping enough hours, having the recommended daily allowance of fruit, vegetables, and water, limiting our animal products, being mobile and active daily, and taking some supplements to boost our immune systems, and fight aging and infection. All these only help the body with the smaller part of our general health. Loneliness is the main reason for all deadly illnesses.

We have learned, for hundreds of years, to put ourselves under huge amounts of stress to do what others are expecting from us, and not to do what we love to do. We expect to do what is required to be done, being controlled by who we are, what we must achieve, and when. We are not allowed to be ourselves. We are expected to wear masks from the time we wake up, changing mask after mask, all day long.

If you want to live happier and longer, and be free of illness, you need to learn how to do what you like, and what is important and useful for yourself, first.

No doubt, we must do physical activities and eat well. We need healthy relationships and the best professional lives. We need to express creatively, be spiritually connected, be healthy financially, live in a healthy environment, be mentally healthy, and of course, all the things we traditionally associate with health—all these things nurture the body.

Not only, you need to know what healthy food and drink is, but you also need to know the real you. When you respect your needs, and yourself as you are, then you can make positive changes, live healthier, and enjoy your education, work, and life, and be happier. There are an unbelievable number of studies and articles on psychological literature and sociological literature.

Although there is lots of evidence in The New England Journal of Medicine and in The Journal of the American Medical Association, many came out of Harvard, Yale, and Johns Hopkins. This is real data, proving that being stress free helps you to heal yourself. It is so important to do this healing now, without any delay. All the world's nations are falling down, and actions must start to be taken in each home. You need to love yourself and have faith that you can do it. Stop believing in the impossible; delete it from your mind.

Connection and Commutation for Healing

Our nervous systems are created in a way that requires human connection, so when we feel socially isolated, our nervous system goes into threat mode, putting us at risk of any kind of illness, when the nervous system is in fight or flight response, the body starts filling itself with cortisol and epinephrine. These hormones put us at risk of heart disease and so many other kinds of illness.

Do you remember how many times you got ill, hours or days after being upset for any reason?

Your body is beautifully equipped with natural self-healing mechanisms. In everyday life, you can fight illness caused by the environment, food, or any other reasons. We have natural longevity enhancements built into our bodies. Those natural self-healing mechanisms only work when the nervous system is in the relaxation response. This is the parasympathetic nervous system. When we know we are an important part of the community, and when we can feel that we are loved and accepted, as in a tribe, then the nervous system relaxes and feels secure enough to fight any outside threat, from whatever illness. Studies show that meditation, yoga, and prayer could reduce the need for health care services by 43%, giving you time to grow and to enjoy your time.

If you and I managed to heal ourselves and our families, and have a positive effect on our close friends and everybody connected with us, we could live healthier and be more able to look after our families. We could enjoy every minute of our lives, and there would be less stress in the world.

Many other studies have shown that eliciting the relaxation response—a physiologic state of deep rest—not only relieves stress and anxiety but also affects physiologic factors, such as blood pressure, heart rate, and oxygen consumption. Imagine if all the blood pressure, heart, and cancer patients learned the effect of connection and being themselves, 15 years before they developed their illness. They could survive, and would be happier, able, and active, and their families would also be healthier.

There are so many conventional and unconventional things affecting our health. The greatest risk factor for our health, which could be the biggest problem in every home, is that each family member might be suffering from loneliness and isolation, despite being together and sharing the same roof. A very interesting study compared the health statistics of Rosetans to neighbouring towns, and the initial results were astonishing. During the seven-year period of study, from 1955–1961:

1. No one in Roseto, under the age of 47, died of a heart attack, and there was a complete absence of heart disease in men under the age of 55.
2. The rate of heart attacks in men over 65 was half the national average.
3. The death rates from all causes, other than old age, were 35% lower than anywhere else.
4. There was no suicide, no alcoholism, no drug addiction, and very little crime.

The study confirmed the doctor's findings, and went on to examine the factors that gave the Rosetans such improved health. It became known as the The Roseto Effect.

The Rosetans had extremely low to no heart disease; yet they ate red meat, deep-fried in lard, smoked and drank heavily, and worked in toxic slate mines. The researchers were totally stumped as well, and they studied all other possible factors, such as ethnicity, water supply, and environment. In the end, the researchers concluded that the unusually low incidence of heart disease in the town could not be attributed to any of these factors.

While living in the town to conduct the study, however, the researchers observed several major differences as to how the Rosetans related to others in their community. They noticed a remarkably close-knit social pattern that was cohesive and mutually supportive with strong family and community ties, where the elderly, in particular, were not marginalized but revered. Simply, the Rosetans lived in brotherhood with one another, and had unconditional love and respect. Each one felt that they had responsibilities and duties, just as they had rights. Happily, they respected and supported each other, and these people were dying of old age. That's it: they were never lonely.

But sadly, in 1971, when the new generation decided to copy western life by moving away to live their own dream of the Western life, away from their community, they had the first heart attack recorded, and the first-ever death of somebody less than 45. In less than 10 years, at the end of the 1970s, the number of fatal heart attacks in Roseto matched the national average of neighbouring stats.

Human beings nourish each other, and the health of the body reflects this. Let's learn to create new communities like the old Roseto communities, within our families and societies, by building a small social network to create better futures for ourselves and new generations. When a child first learns to move around, he tries to touch and discover everything around him, but we tell him no, and to stop and not do it, and that it is wrong, shameful, and unaccepted, even when there is no risk or damage. If the child could enjoy his everyday adventures and freedom to discover the world around him, he would only need love and support, instead of being taught to be controlled. When he grows up, he would do the same with any other child.

We come to this world from love, and when we die, we must go back to love.

The Secret of Why Blue Zone Populations Live Longer and Healthier Lives

In November 2005, National Geographic magazine covered the story, "The Secrets of a Long Life," by Dan Buettner. He claims that there is an unusual number of people living to be greater than 100, in the Blue Zones regions, He identified five areas: Okinawa (Japan), Sardinia (Italy), Nicoya (Costa Rica), Icaria (Greece), and Loma Linda (California). He offers an explanation, based on data and first-hand observations, as to why these populations live healthier and longer lives.

Elders in Okinawa, Japan, one of the original Blue Zones longevity hotspots, live extraordinarily better and longer lives than almost anyone else in the world. They have what is called Moai, which is one of their traditional longevity social support groups, and it starts in childhood and extends throughout the 100 years. The term originated hundreds of years ago as a means of a village's financial support system. They survived world war despite all the historic complications, which link to emotional, financial, social, and health damages. Originally, moais were Mind Over Medicine, by Lissa Rankin

The Moai groups formed to pool the resources of an entire village for projects or public works. If an individual needed capital to buy land or take care of an emergency, the only way was to pool money locally. Today, the idea has expanded to become more of a social support network and a cultural tradition for built-in companionship.

They meet regularly, sometimes daily or a couple of days a week, to gossip, talk about their life experiences, and to share advice and even financial assistance when needed. They all give and take.

Traditionally, children from the age of five years old are paired together. They make a commitment to each other for life; they do not allow anything to break their circle; they build strong loyalty to each other, as strong as family relationships (maybe better than most of the world's families in the world). They would meet regularly with their Moai, for both work and play, and to pool resources. Some Moais have lasted over 90 years!

It isn't just about gossip and chatting; it's a strong support and network for each other. Each member counts on each other. If one gets sick, or a spouse dies, or they run out of money, they know someone will step in and help.

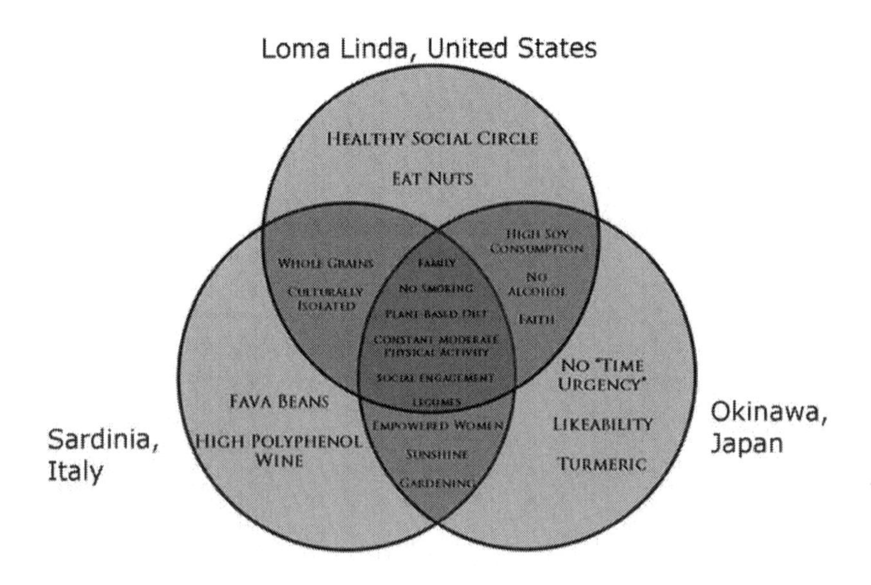

The above is a Venn diagram of longevity clues from Okinawa, Sardinia, and Loma Linda, which could allow us to learn from them.

As you can see from the Venn diagram, their power to live longer and healthier came from the fact that:

1. They empowered their women, and gave them leadership.
2. They enjoy the sunshine.
3. The gardening work is part of their life.
4. They have huge respect for the family, and support each other, and do not let any misunderstandings or mistakes, from any member, to break them apart.
5. They do not smoke.
6. They depend on a plant diet, legumes, and social engagement.

It's much easier to go through life knowing there is a safety net, than being alone.

It is so easy, and it should not be harder than our recent, unreal and fake lifestyle. If we follow in their footsteps, we will live longer, healthier, and happier lives. We need to love ourselves first, as we are, to unconditionally respect each other and to be connected with each other—yes, connected. We need to start creating, just as the Moai and Rosata groups did, for others, and ourselves, and for our children. No doubt, each one of us wants the best for our children, but we first need to learn to accept ourselves as we are, and accept the challenges as a positive opportunity to learn in order to grow every day. We need to teach our children how to care for themselves and others, have a group understanding, and rely on each other in crisis, with mutual respect from a young age. It is so important; we need to build on our society groups, as Moais groups, and rely on each other—not on money in the bank, a house, land, or beauty.

We urgently need to be reconnected with each other, with less worry and stress—connected with unconditional love and respect, for everyone.

We are created to be part of each other, not to be isolated or separated from each other, or even isolated from ourselves. This is why our nervous system is not stable. It is in threat response most of the time, causing us visible and invisible disease. Our nervous system is in fight or flight response most of the time, and it is confused. It cannot decide if you have a real threat or a socially learned threat, which causes us stress most of our days.

Most of us are separated from our family and loved ones, trying to find happiness and live our dream. By creating our Moais, we could be as successful as the Free Zones regions. Let's organize regular groups.

Most of us are secretly struggling, scared to be ourselves. We are scared to show what we are. Let's put our hands together. This planet belongs to all of us. Let's fix it together. We are all Adam and Eve's grandchildren.

Let's save ourselves and start to take real steps toward change, before it is too late. A study shows: Air pollution increases your mortality by 6%; obesity by 23%; alcohol abuse by 37%; but loneliness increases it by 45%. Loneliness is as dangerous for your health as smoking 15 cigarettes per day.

Another study in Alameda County showed that people with the fewest social ties were 3 times more likely to have died over a 9-year period. There was another study in UCSF, of 3,000 women with breast cancer, which showed that people who go through their cancer journey alone are 4 times more likely to die from their disease than those who have 10 or more friends. Lonely people have higher rates of heart disease, cancer, dementia, high blood pressure, diabetes, infection, anxiety, depression, insomnia, suicide alcoholism, and addictions.

Despite all the studies and the evidence that loneliness affects our physical and mental health, not too much is done to solve it!! Despite all the negative effects on our wellness, not all of us are taking it into account or trying to change. Sadly, our body carries and develops many health problems.

Yet you could feel lonelier in a crowd of people than when you're alone. You need to recognize this and build peace within yourself first. The significant problem is when you feel separated from the people that you love the most. We must all be connected to each other. We all are the grandchildren of Adam and Eve!! We must stop separating ourselves from each other and from our real selves.

The number one barrier to belonging is fitting in. If I'm feeling like I have to pretend to be something that I'm not, in order to fit in with others and be accepted, I'm going to feel lonely, even if I have thousands around me. If only we could change the way we learn to look at each other, and at ourselves, and stop being worried about what people say about us. If only we all could learn from our mistakes, and respect who we really are. If only our slanders and criteria were adjusted by default. For example, you might not have time or money to buy a gift, and you are invited to a wedding, where you are expected to buy a gift for the bride. You might be under huge stress to find money and time to buy a gift that the bride might never need and will not even use. So you put yourself and the family under stress. Let's try to change our lives, and do what we can, when we can. If all of society managed to change, we all would live happier. It could take time, but let's start now. If I change, and you change, all of us will change to our best selves.

Loneliness Prescription

In regard to the loneliness being the main reason for most, if not all, our illnesses, dealing with it and treating it has to be given priority.

So, what is the loneliness prescription?

We need each other. Sometimes you might have difficulties—socially, mentally, financially, and for many other reasons—so it is okay to admit and ask for help from therapists and spiritual counsellors. It is not shameful, and all of us might have this feeling at one stage of our lives. We might manage to recover by ourselves, but sometimes we cannot.

You need to first be friends with yourself. As long as you're at war with yourself— with those inner voices that are telling you that you don't belong, that you're not lovable, that you're not enough, that you don't deserve to be part of a community—you're going to have a hard time being close to the people that are right there to love you.

We have to delete the shame and perfectionism, not just in ourselves but in the communities, and how we relate to each other. If I'm ashamed, and I'm hiding myself from you, and you do the same, or if I think I have to be perfect and I'm not allowed to reveal my vulnerabilities to you, I'm going to separate myself, even if I'm surrounded by people. My nervous system is going to go into threat mode, and it's going to put me at risk of disease. We need to start building a trusted circle for our children and ourselves; we need to rebuild whole communities to learn how we can accept each other for who we are and what we have.

In The Blue Zones, they live longer, healthier, and happier lives than the rest of the world, because the social support group is an important component of all the five Blue Zones cultures. Social connectedness is ingrained, and it is as important for them as breathing and drinking water to live. Imagine how much we miss in our busy lives, especially with the new complicated and fast technology. It separated us even more.

We need to teach the generations to build social networks, and how to be themselves, without worrying about how they are on the outside. They need to build a group of lifelong friends, and continue to be connected with a social support group that is formed in order to provide varying support from social, financial, health, or spiritual interests. It's much easier to go through life knowing there is a safety net to lean on when you need it. To enjoy being connected is the biggest step for healing.

So much medical data shows evidence that relationships matter. People who have a strong social network have half the rate of heart disease compared to those who are lonely. Married people are two times likely to live a longer life than unmarried people. In fact, curing your loneliness may be the most important measure of prevention you can enact upon your body. Your spiritual life also matters. People who attend religious services live up to fourteen years longer. Your professional life matters as well.

The people who fail to take a vacation are actually three times more likely to get heart disease. Your attitude really matters. Happy people live 7–10 years longer than unhappy people. Optimists are 77% less likely to get heart disease than the pessimist.

Your brain communicates with all the cells in your body, via hormones and neurotransmitters. For example, if you have a negative thought or feeling, your brain triggers this as a threat, and that something is wrong. So if you feel lonely or pessimistic, or you have problems at work, or you are in a toxic relationship, the amygdala says, "Threat, threat!" It then turns on the hypothalamus to talk to the pituitary gland, which communicates with the adrenal gland, and the adrenal gland starts spitting out stress hormones like cortisol, norepinephrine, and epinephrine. It turns on what Walter Cannon, at Harvard, called the stress response, which triggers the sympathetic nervous system and puts you into fight or fight mode. It is adaptive, and it is protective. For example, if you are about to kill a child while you're driving your car, it is okay for you to have that quick stress response. Then, afterwards, it is supposed to switch right off, but this isn't what happens in our regular lives these days. Fortunately, there is a counter balancing relaxation response, and when this comes about, the stress response turns off. The parasympathetic nervous system turns on, and healing comes from oxytocin dopamine, nitric oxide, and endorphins, which fill the body and bathe every cell in the body. It is a natural self-repair mechanism that we all have, but they only turn on when the nervous system is relaxed. So when you have stress responses, all those natural self-repair mechanisms get flipped off, and the body is too busy trying to fight or take flight, in order to heal itself.

Stress Is the Main Reason for Our Illness

Stress is the stronger reason for creating illness, but why is it not taken into consideration, despite it being the main reason for a lot of the world's illnesses? Is it because, deep inside us, we all worry about facing ourselves?

You need to start questioning yourself about what went wrong in your life. Was it a toxic relationship? Was it refusal to do work that you must do to earn money to survive? Is it guilt...??

We take painkillers, or visit our doctor to get medication to fix us so we can go back to our life game. It is the same as a football player in football games: if he gets injured, the physiotherapist, doctor, and OT take him out for a few minutes to fix his injury, and then they put him back in the game. Many players, after they retire, end up with so many health problems. Perhaps the football player should get out of any game after his injuries, instead of being fixed and sent back to the game.

We are filling our bodies with medication to stay on our feet and survive, and to stay in the life game. Our test results could show negative, and that there is nothing wrong with us, but to continue in our life game, we could ask our doctor for medication to relieve our symptoms, without treating the real cause of our illness—medications that are silently damaging our kidneys, liver, and heart.

Our nervous system has two operating systems. There's the fight or flight stress response (sympathetic nervous system), and there is the parasympathetic nervous system, or what Herbert Benson, at Harvard, called the relaxation response.

Stress is normal when your life is at risk, or if your child is bleeding heavily, and you have no access to medical help, or if you're stuck in the lift with your children, and the power is cut for an hour and you cannot press the alarm button. Stress is also caused by social isolation and loneliness.

Stress is selling you for a paycheck. Stress is a pessimistic worldview. Stress is fearful, anxious, worried thoughts. Stress is toxic relationships. Stress is money worries. Stress is knowing that you have a demand within you that you have yet to get out of you. Stress is feeling out of touch with your life's purpose. Stress is negative beliefs about your health. Stress is overwhelming. Stress is feeling like nobody really gets to know the real you. Stress is pretending to be something that you're not. Stress is feeling disconnected from source.

Lots of us have said that we were misunderstood, and we couldn't explain ourselves, or the reason that we were scared. We were too worried to express exactly who we are, or what was in our mind.

On average, in the 21st century, we have more than 50 stress responses per day, in our modern culture, and every time the body is in stress response, its natural self-repair mechanisms are disabled and confused. You develop illness as a result, and then you make your way to a doctor after your body fails to heal. Mostly, doctors deal with your symptoms; they are not able to deal with the real stress. So both of you are unable to recognize the signs, to identify what went wrong and activated those stress responses in your body.

Most of the time, doctors end up giving you medication to deal with your symptoms, as you complain about symptoms of instability, but if you slow down, you could give yourself the opportunity to heal yourself. Taking too much medication could reduce your life expectancy and the quality of your life. Medication could disable your natural self-repair mode, so you need to learn the best ways to find the real you, and deal with stress in a better way.

There is scientific proof that you can heal yourself, and there is lots of scientific data that proves how stress affects our bodies.

Stress is anything that triggers the amygdala in your brain to turn on what is called the stress response, which is also known as the fight or flight response. So, anything that turns on your fight or flight response, puts you into the sympathetic nervous system and fills your body with cortisol, epinephrine, and other very poisonous stress hormones. It is normal if you are getting chased by a tiger, because it helps to protect your life.

But your amygdala doesn't know the difference between really being in a dangerous situation, or if it is only negative thoughts, beliefs, and feelings that originate in your mind, which turn on those stress responses.

Our nervous system has two operating systems. There's the fight or flight stress response—the sympathetic nervous system. And there is the parasympathetic nervous system, or what is called the relaxation response.

Chronic stress should not be an inevitable part of our lives. We need to learn from the Blue Zones regions around the world—those parts of the world where there is a greater than average percentage of people who live to be over 100. These people know what soul medicine is, and they manage to be themselves and accept others as they are.

So, what is the medicine that we really need?

Medicine is being loved, just as we are, without the need to keep changing masks. Medicine is helping those in need, close to us and around the world. Medicine is expressing your creative genius. Medicine is to find your talent, and to make it shine. Medicine is always seeing the glass half-full. Medicine is the unconditional love for each other, animals, and the world around us. Medicine is being able to show your happiness everywhere, all the time, without the need for caffeine and alcohol. Medicine is speaking your truth. Medicine is a belief that you belong. Medicine is communing with nature. Medicine is nourishing the body with real food. Medicine is tapping in the source. Medicine is being, unapologetically, you.

You need a real therapist who can achieve healing you without causing you any harm, and yet when you look at the causes of death, preventable medical error is the third leading cause of death, according to the Centre for Disease Control and the Institute of Medicine. And it's not just medical error; it's the whole nature of our pill-popping medical culture, which has been adopted by patients and doctors alike. Stress is one of the biggest killers among us, and dealing with it at an early stage is the best vaccination.

You can heal yourself, before you fall victim to any illness, find the medicine that you really need. Healing yourself will lead to healing your family. It will heal your children and protect them from what you went through. Celebrate your success as soon as you step out of negativity, to any small improvement of being better, on any field. Celebrate your partner's positivity, your child's experiment, the farmer, the cleaner, your friend, and your parents' movements.

Humanely nourish each other. You will get higher energy when you are validating others, especially when you give it with love and passion. Love yourself, and everybody will love and care for you.

Mind and the Placebo Effect on Healing

The scientific community and the medical establishment have been proving for over 50 years that the mind can heal the body. They studied what is called the placebo effect. The placebo is a thorn in the side of medical establishment. It is the inconvenient truth that gets in between trying to bring new treatments and new surgeries into the medical establishment. But I want to help you to use the placebo to heal yourself and your beloved children and family, saving yourselves from the massive side effects of any medication you could be prescribed via your doctor. The placebo effect is excellent news because it's concrete evidence that the body holds innate self-repair mechanisms within itself, which can make unthinkable things happen to the body. If you find this surprising, and if you have a hard time believing that the body can heal itself, you need to look no further than the Spontaneous Remission Project, which is a database compiled by The Institute of Noetic Sciences, of over 3500 case studies, in the medical literature of patients who have gotten better from seemingly incurable illnesses. Have a look at the databases, and you will be really surprised: stage 4 cancer that disappeared without treatment; HIV positive results that became negative; heart disease, kidney failure, diabetes, high blood pressure, thyroid disease, and autoimmune diseases—gone.

A great example of this, in the medical literature, is a case study from 1957, of Mr. Wright, who had advanced lymphosarcoma. He had tumours the size of oranges in his armpit, neck, chest, abdomen, and lungs, but he was not giving up hope. He had heard about this wonder drug, called Krebiozen, and he was begging his doctor to give it to him. Unfortunately, the Krebiozen was only available if the patient had at least three months to live. But Mr. Wright was tenacious and did not give up. He kept badgering his doctor until he finally agreed to give it to him. So Dr. West dosed him up on Friday, not expecting that Mr. Wright would make it through the weekend, but to his utter shock, when he came to do rounds on Monday, Mr. Wright was up walking around the ward, and his tumours had shrunk to half of their original size. They had melted like snowballs on a hot stove, and ten days later, they were all gone. This lasted for two months, until the initial report came out about Krebiozen, which said that it did not really look like Krebiozen was working. So Mr. Wright fell into deep depression, and the cancer came back. This time, Dr. West decided to get sneaky, and he told his patient that the Krebiozen that he had before was a tainted version. He told him that he now had some ultrapure, highly concentrated Krebiozen. He then injected Mr. Wright with nothing but distilled water, and once again, the tumours disappeared, and the fluid in his lungs went away. Mr. Wright was up rocking and rolling for another two months, and then the American Medical Association blew it by publishing a nationwide study that proved definitively that Krebiozen was worthless. Two days later, Mr. Wright, after hearing this news, died.

This case study is a great example of the placebo effect, and its opposite, the nocebo effect. So Mr. Wright got that distilled water, and his tumours melted away. That is a great example of the placebo effect, when you get a seemingly inert treatment, and yet something is happening physiologically in the body, such that the disease goes away. The nocebo effect is also effective.

Three baby girls were delivered by a midwife on Friday the 13th, in Okefenokee Swamp, near the Georgia-Florida border, and the midwife pronounced that these three babies, born on such a fateful day, were all hexed. She said the first would die before her 16th birthday, the second before her 21st birthday, and the third before her 23rd birthday. As it turned out, the first girl died the day before her 16th birthday; the second died before her 21st birthday; and the third, when she got wind of what happened to the other two, the day before her 23rd birthday, showed up at the hospital, hyperventilating and begging them to make sure she survived. She wound up dying that night.

These two case studies were part of thousands of case studies, and they are great examples of the placebo effect and its opposite, the nocebo effect. Mr. Wright, when he got that distilled water, and his tumour melted away, was a great example of the placebo effect, where you get a seemingly inert treatment, and yet something is happening physiologically in the body, such that disease goes away.

The nocebo effect is the opposite. So, the three hexed girls were an example of the nocebo effect: the mind's belief that something bad is going to happen in the body. The scientific literature medical journals, like the New England Journal of Medicine, and the Journal of the American Medical Association, are full of evidence that the placebo effect and the nocebo effect are incredibly powerful. There is much evidence since the 1950s, and there are countless case studies that show, in almost all studies, if you give people a fake treatment—a sugar pill, a saline injection, or most effective, a fake surgery—it is recorded that between 50–80% of the time, the patient gets better, and it's not just in their mind. It is not only that they're just feeling better; they're thinking better. It's actually in their physiology, and this is measurable. So, for example, when patients get placebos, it was found that ulcers healed, colons became less inflamed, bronchi dilated, warts disappeared, and cells looked different under the microscope. It is provable, and it is happening in the body, even though it's initiated by the mind. So when you look at these, some of the studies are just amazing, like the Rogain studies. They got a bunch of bald men, gave them placebos, and they grew hair.

The opposite is also true. So, if you give people a placebo, and you tell them it is chemotherapy, they vomit and they lose their hair, so this is really happening in the body. The question is, is it just the mind's positive belief that's making this happen?

Using a placebo helps to force healing, not fear or pessimism.

So, if your doctor tells you that you have an incurable illness, you are going to have to take that medication for the rest of your life; or, God forbid, you get cancer, and you have a 5%, five-year survival rate, it is really no different than when that midwife told those three baby girls that they were hexed. It is a form of medical hexing that's so prevalent.

In order to heal ourselves, we need more than just visiting the doctor to become optimally healthy; we need more than just a good diet, a regular exercise program, getting enough vitamins and enough sleep, and following our doctor's orders.

Those things are all great, and critical and important, but we must learn how to live a healthy professional life, a healthy creative life, a healthy spiritual life, a healthy sexual life, and a healthy financial life, all in a healthy environment. In essence, we need a healthy mind. The medical literature has more than enough data to prove that all of those things are essential, so what are we waiting for?

Healing Your Heart Heals Your Life

Sometimes you have a voice that says, "I must be better than I am now." You need to build unconditional love for yourself. Do not wait until you are perfect. Do not wait to improve your income or change your shape. You need to start doing what you want, when you wish to do it, so you will be able to feel the effects of happiness, which increases your motivation to achieve more. You will be able to do this, one step at a time. Stop looking behind, and do not let mistakes frustrate you or pull you down. Keeping your energy up helps you to reach the level of being able to do what you enjoy, which has a great effect on your achievement every day.

Keep your energy up: to strengthen your energy, make at least a small, positive change regularly. Sometimes you have a lot on your plate. Do not compare yourself with others, unless you are aiming to make a positive change, and you are building a good self-understanding. As the Dalai Lama said: "The secret for happiness is doing more of what you love, and less of what you don't love, every day."

Avoid negative thinking and negative people: It could be easy to step away from negative people, but it is harder if these people are family members. You are almost obligated to go the extra mile for the sake of the integrity of the family group. If you don't get along with a family member, it may very well put stress and strain on you, and it affects family relationships as well. Stay calm when you feel yourself starting to get irritated by someone; slow down, breathe deeply, and accept the difficult person as he is. Try to avoid flaring up the relationship; give yourself permission to take care of your needs, and listen to your body and do not push yourself to accept what your mind and body are rejecting. If the low energy people are not part of your close family, step back from them until you reach complete self-healing. Negativity can lower your immune system, and destroy your mental and emotion state, but high-energy people, with their high energy and passion, make you more able to enjoy creativity. Achieving this level is one of the big, important steps in your life, to keep you healthy and help you succeed in all levels of your life.

Chapter 2

The Relationship Between Sleeping and Healing

Sleeping and the Effect on Your General Health

Sleeping plays an important role in your physical health. Lack of sleep causes many preventable illnesses and problems: trouble with concentration, memory problems, mood instability, being prone to accidents, weakening your immunity, high blood pressure, increasing the risk of diabetes, weight gain, lower sex drive, poor balance, and deficiencies that are linked to an increased risk of heart disease, kidney disease, high blood pressure, diabetes, and stroke.

Sleeping Affects Your Brain and Memory

When you do not have enough sleep, your brain cells become unable to communicate effectively, which, in turn, can lead to temporary mental lapses that affect your memory and vision, as well as causing many other health, social, and financial problems. You may be more likely to be forgetful and get distracted more easily, which affects your communication skills and achievements. While medical solutions for memory loss remain elusive, but the healthy diet, and the physical activities , socialization, and lifelong learning can push back cognitive impairment.

Sleepiness Changes Your Appetite

Maintaining a healthy diet isn't easy if you're not getting enough sleep. During sleep deprivation, your body releases higher amounts of the hunger hormone while releasing less of the satiety hormone, leptin. The appetite changes continue, as the body craves unhealthy foods when you're tired. When you eat these foods, your brain gets more rewards than usual, causing you to crave them even more. Appetite changes are one of the reasons that prolonged sleep deprivation may lead to unwanted weight gain and diabetes.

The Immune System and Sleeping

While you are asleep, your immune system gets to work, recharging itself and making antibodies. If you get less than seven hours of sleep, you're 2.94 times more likely to develop a cold, and you are victim to many other illnesses. When you get sick, the immune system that is depressed by sleep deprivation takes longer to fight off infection.

Your immune system and health can also be impacted by poor sleep quality. The immune system goes to work recharging itself and fighting infection while you're in the deepest levels of sleep. If the sleeping time becomes shorter, or you experience sleep disturbances during the night, the immune system doesn't get enough time needed to stay healthy.

Your body needs to sleep as much as it needs air and food, to function at its best. During sleep, your body heals itself and restores its chemical balance. Your brain forges new connections, and this helps memory retention. But without enough sleep, your brain and body systems won't function normally. It can also dramatically lower your quality of life. A review of 16 studies found that sleeping for less than 6 to 8 hours a night increases the risk of early death by about 12%. Chronic sleep deprivation can interfere with your body's internal systems, and cause more than just the initial signs and symptoms listed above.

Ways to Improve Your Sleeping Habits

Increase bright light exposure during the day. Natural sunlight or bright light during the day helps keep your circadian rhythm healthy. This improves daytime energy, as well as night-time sleep quality and duration. People with insomnia, who had daytime bright light exposure, improved sleep quality and duration.

Reduce blue light exposure in the evening. Exposure to light during the day is beneficial, but night-time light exposure has the opposite effect. This is due to its impact on your circadian rhythm. It is like tricking your brain into thinking it is still daytime, and this reduces hormones, like melatonin, which help you relax and get deep sleep.

There are several popular methods you can use to reduce night-time blue light exposure. These include wearing glasses that block blue light, not watching TV, and turning off any bright lights two hours before heading to bed.

Avoid consuming caffeine in the afternoon. A single dose of caffeine can enhance focus, energy, and sports performance, but if it is consumed late in the day, caffeine stimulates your nervous system and may stop your body from naturally relaxing at night.

Caffeine can stay elevated in your blood for 6 to 8 hours.

Reduce irregular or long daytime naps. Short naps generally don't affect night- time sleep quality for most people. But if you experience insomnia or poor sleep quality at night, napping might worsen these problems. Long or frequent naps might interfere with night-time sleep.

Don't Drink Alcohol. Downing a couple of drinks at night can negatively affect your sleep, and your hormones. Alcohol is known to cause, or increase, the symptoms of sleep apnea, snoring, and disrupted sleep patterns. It also alters night- time melatonin production.

In general, alcohol has a massive, negative impact on your health. Avoiding it will be much better for you.

Chapter 3

The Effect of Meditation on Parenting

The New You

Having a new baby is a transformational process that brings changes in every aspect of a woman's life. The transition to motherhood comprises of developmental tasks, including taking responsibility for the child day and night; forming a bond with the baby; adapting to changing relationships with the partner and everybody around her; forming a mother's identity; searching for answers to unending questions about parenting, childhood, and children's health; trying to find balance with other activities; and learning motherhood duties.

Learning mothering encompasses an endless list of abilities, including regulating the baby's emotional, mental, and health states, and the mother's own emotional reactions to the demands of the baby.

Parenting is also immensely rewarding and nourishing, but it can also be very stressful, with non-stop emotional changes.

Healing Yourself Is the Key to Successful Parenting

I am sure that virtually all of us were wounded in one way or another when we were children. The biggest problem is that most of us either do not recognise the need for meditation and healing, or we recognise it but are unable to admit that our childhood pulled us down because of the relationship and bad experiences.

In fact, if we don't heal those wounds, they do not allow us to parent our children optimally. If there's an area where you were scared as a child, this scar could cause you instability, and puts you in the state of fight or flight, causing you unnecessary, stressful responses, which wounds your child too.

Each one of us wants to be the best parent for our children. We need to give more attention, and notice where we overreact.

No doubt, you do not want to repeat your painful childhood history with your kids. Avoiding the fight or flight stress response, if you're already well down the wrong path, is the most important thing in your life. I am sure that you wish to be in the relaxation responses, and to stop causing your children pain as a result of your unhealed wounds.

Take a deep breath. You already got out from that hard childhood, and you are healed from such a hard experience. It is just a bad memory that is left behind, which you can clear out; so, slow down, and take time off. You need to avoid doing what could cause you to feel sorry later, if you do not slow down.

When we get angry, we might overreact. We could say things and act in a way in which we would not normally do, if we were given the choice while our emotions were in a better state. The reason is that your body and emotions are in fight or flight mode most of the time, and it could seem to you that your child is the main reason for you being irritated, and causes you instability. Slow down, take deep breaths, get away if possible, and take your time to calm down.

You can't change the fact that you had a painful childhood. That is the past, but you are able to change those feelings, your thinking, and the effect of such a hard childhood on your present life and children. If any of your parents, or adults in your life, hurt or abandoned you, which made you feel that you weren't good enough, the time has come to put yourself in their shoes. From your adult vantage point, you can understand now that you were more than enough. A more accurate understanding would be that your parents were frightened. They had their own difficult and painful childhood, with enough negative effects on their lives, which put them in the state of fight or flight most of the time, when they gave you that negative feeling about yourself. Each of us is born with beauty, and we are smart, creative, and able, and our children are too, but our bad experiences from our childhood could be affecting us. Do not let your children be affected too. Put it right, and allow yourself a space of healing and peace within yourself, to create peace around you.

Forgiveness is the best way to live in peace with yourself and others,. You do not need to repeat history and cause your children pain like you had, or at a different level or shape.

When you understand the mechanism of the emotions, you will understand how to deal with your bad memories, and you will manage to continue healing your life.

Our children don't need perfection from us, but they need us to meet their physical, emotional, and intellectual needs. Trust their abilities, support them, and give them unconditional love as they are.

The Best Way To Meditate

The following relaxation technique is based on the progressive muscle relaxation technique that Dr. Edmund Jacobson developed in the 1920s. It will help you alleviate tension.

Sit down in a place where you feel relaxed and comfortable, and close your eyes.

Take a few deep, cleansing breaths as you begin to relax. Bring all of your attention to your breath, and slow it down, taking deep inhales and slow exhales.

Make your mind follow your breathing, no matter what; focus your mind on the breath, and follow as the breath inhales and exhales.

Count your breaths at the end of every exhale. Don't let your mind count before the end of the exhale. The mind always wants to jump ahead, but take the control and don't allow it. Your mind has to remain focused on being the follower.

Count to 10, slowly, and always at the end of each exhale, continuing to let the mind follow the breath. Bring all of your attention to your right foot, noticing how it feels. Squeeze the right foot, and all five toes; tense and squeeze it tightly. Hold this tension for two deep breaths.

Then, suddenly release all tension in the right foot. Relax it completely, and notice the tension release. You may feel a tingling sensation in the foot.

Move your attention to your left foot. Follow the same instructions as you had for the right foot.

Move slowly up and around the body, squeezing one body part at a time to create tension, immediately followed by the contrasting sensation of release and ease. Follow each part with a deep, cleansing breath. Here's a sample progression you can follow:

- Right foot, left foot
- Right ankle and calf, left ankle and calf
- Right knee, left knee
- Right thigh, left thigh
- Both feet and legs
- Hips
- Butt
- Belly
- Entire lower body, from the tummy down
- Chest and heart
- Right arm, left arm
- Right hand, left hand
- Shoulders
- Neck
- Face
- Whole body at once

Parents Group Meditation

Some new mothers perceive that due to the demands, it might be difficult to deal with such stress alone, and some might be unable to concentrate, or to relax and meditate with the available coping resources. The stress experience could drive her to a level of chronic mental health problems in any stage of her life, as it happens to lots of mothers.

Some mothers, and some fathers, might not be able to relax and do meditation by themselves. At this stage, they need support.

Through meditation experts, family counselors, or individual/group discussions with other parents who have the same difficulties, they can hear and discuss each other's experiences, and have short mindfulness practice.

Healing Yourself Is Vital for Your Children's Successful Lives

Some parents, as soon as they have children, will be stressed out about how they can fit their children into the community from a very young age. Parents express their stress and worry, putting their children under unnecessary stress. Most parents feel that their kids cannot be successful unless they are protecting and preventing at every turn, hovering over every happening, micromanaging every moment, and steering their kids toward some small subset of colleges and careers. When we raise our kids this way, the kids end up leading a kind of check-listed childhood, where parents believe that they must keep them safe and sound, and fed and watered. Then they want to be sure that they go to the right schools, and have the right classes at the right schools. They must get the right grades in the right classes in the right schools. They tell their kids to not just join a club but to start a club, because college wants to see that, and they can check the box off for community service. They care about others, and all of this is done while hoping for a degree of perfection.

They expect their kids to perform at a level of perfection that they were never asked to perform at themselves, causing the children to be stressed, worried, and depressed. Regardless of where they end up at the end of high school, they are breathless, a little burned out, and they are a little old before their time, wishing the grown-ups in their lives had said: What you have done is enough. They are withering now under a high rate of anxiety and depression, wondering if this life is worth it, while they still have a long way to go to achieve what is expected from them. They put their talents on the back burner, wishing the grown-ups had asked them to do what they naturally love, instead of taking their attention away from what they enjoy.

You need to learn to live in peace with yourself, and to take care of yourself first, in order to manage and take care of your kids. It does not mean to be selfish. In fact, it will help you to demonstrate to your children that self-care is important. When you create time for yourself, you will be more able to handle the parenting stress. The result is a relaxed, loving environment for all of you as a family. Your children will be happier and more capable, and connected with the family and with other happy children. This will help them to grow in a safe loving environment, have healthy relationships via being connected with healthy relationships, and to find their creativity and successes in their life.

When you make time to take care of yourself, it enables you to be compassionate with yourself, and to more compassionate towards your children and teenagers.

Unconditional love and trust is what most children in this world are missing. Let's heal ourselves, to create happiness for ourselves and everybody around us.

Your Child Erases Your Childhood Pain

Being a parent gives you the greatest opportunity to heal yourself. Most parents say that loving their children has transformed them, by making them more patient, more compassionate, more selfless, and optimised. Loving your children helps you to heal those unloved places inside you. In fact, if we pay attention, our children have an unerring ability to show us our wounded places. Our children draw out our unreasonable fears and angers. Being parents gives us the perfect opportunity to grow and heal. Most of us run away from this hard inner work, but there is nothing better than our kids' smiles to motivate us to live our best possible lives. It is almost magical. As our wounds transform, we find that these hurt places inform us and motivate us, driving us to be better parents and happier people.

In the next chapter, you will be shocked and surprised at how you are killing yourself and your family by consuming unhealthy food, which we have learned, for many years, is not good for us. We must respond to the wakeup call before it is too late, and make lots of changes in our lives.

Chapter 4

War Against Artificial Food

The History of Shifting to Processed Food

In 1960, there was discussion of an impending global pandemic of obesity, which was thought of as heresy.

At the beginning of the 1970s, the world happily shifted toward the increased reliance upon processed foods, which took away from home cooking, and made greater use of edible oils and sugar-sweetened beverages. Smoking, reduced physical activity, and increased sedentary time were seen also. These changes began in the early 1990s, in the low and middle-income world, but did not become clearly recognized until diabetes, hypertension, and obesity began to dominate the globe. It then quickly started to hit most homes.

As a result of the greedy, misleading food marketing, in the last four or five generations, adults committed the biggest mistake in history. They were providing their beloved children (us) with food and drink that was shortening their lifespan. It was causing uncountable medical, emotional, and mental problems as a result of such food. We urgently need to start making changes in our lifestyle in regard to how we are living, and with the food we eat; otherwise, children will live a life ten years shorter than their parents, on top of lowering the quality of their lives.

As you are no doubt aware, the quality of your life and health is less than your parents as a result of the landscape of food that we built around ourselves, on top of all the other negative effects of the many global changes. IT technology has positive advantages, but there are also many hidden disadvantages of the screens in our lives; yet there are lots of studies that need to be done to find out how we can prevent the damage, which is a result of the screen effects in our life.

The statistic of bad health is clear. Even so, we spend our lives being paranoid about death (which we see on the front of every newspaper), ignoring the diet-related disease. All of us know that diet-related disease is the biggest killer in the world. It is a global problem, which needs to be solved and to be a priority.

The Global Budget for Diseases Related to Food

The usual figure given by Public Health England (PHE) for the cost of obesity in England is £6.1bn per year. But to make this claim clearer, McKinsey has combined the cost of obesity with the cost of diabetes. It breaks the figures down into £6bn in the UK, for obesity, and others related to food disease, to £10bn, for the cost of treating.

Diabetes in the USA accounts for 10% of the healthcare bills. There is 150 billion dollars spent on food-related diseases a year, and this is still rising every year. It is a really big problem that needs to be addressed.

The world is spending 2 trillion dollars annually on obesity, according to a new report, which is more than the combined costs of armed violence, war, and terrorism.

Our children are the fourth and fifth generations that have not grown up in a real food environment. Children around the world do not know the name of most of the local fruits and vegetables, so how can we expect them to eat healthy? They haven't been taught to cook at home or in the school. They are not taught why processed food is bad for them. As a result of the unhealthy eating, it is hard for them to concentrate on their education!! Most of their food is largely processed and full of all sorts of additives and extra ingredients. Promotion and size is obviously the massive problem nowadays. Food is a most dangerous enemy, masked by a loving face.

Forty - fifty years ago, food was grown in soil (fruit, vegetables, and seeds), and fish, meat, and chicken were free-range and used to be consumed in smaller amounts and occasionally.

Forty-fifty years after the massive food factories started preparing our food, most of us had fallen victim to our loving parents, who believed and trusted human-made food.

We need to listen to the wakeup call, and nourish our children with real food. To save their lives, and the upcoming generation's lives, they must get the right food. They must learn how to be themselves, and they need to be provided with harmony and love.

It could be that most of your unhealthy, unhappy life was a result of the harmful, artificial food. You need to learn, with your children, what real food is. Your children are the fourth and fifth generations affected by the bad food industry.

Parents, these days, are killing their kids slowly by offering them the fast, refined food, which is causing them many health, mental, emotional, and even financial problems. As a result, they are learning and growing up with damaged eating. Children, nowadays, are losing a big part of their lives as a result of suffering from symptoms of illness, which could be prevented but is making them unable to enjoy their childhood.

Re-educate yourself and your children about what real food is, and why you need to heal yourself. Let's put our hands together and get out of this war against the noxious food. We need to overcome the difficulties that we were blinded by for decades.

Finding the real you, along with food education, is important for a happy, successful family.

Food education must be a life skill for all students and young parents—rich or poor, single or married. No matter what the financial difficulties are, it should not matter when it comes to healthy food and a healthy life, as long as the outcome is living longer, healthier, and happier.

We have to put back what has been lost in the last decades.

We must start a lasting and sustainable movement to educate every child about food. Families need to be inspired to cook again. To empower people everywhere to fight obesity, cooking time must be the nicest, most enjoyable and most privileged time of the day. Spending time cleaning and cutting the vegetables, and organizing healthy recipes, is a great experience for the whole family.

Accelerating the Obesity

Forty to fifty years ago, we used to eat more complex food that was less refined, and we exercised more and had heavier duties. The adults used to have activities that helped them to burn the extra fat and lose weight.

There are numerous studies that suggest so many reasons for today's adults having difficulty maintaining the same weight as their counterparts, two to three decades ago, even when the amount of food and exercise are equal.

The adult (30–39 years old) who eats 2,000 calories per day, and exercises two hours per week, is likely to be about

10% heavier than someone of the same age in the 1980s, who followed the same lifestyle habits.

What are the reasons behind that big change?

It was a surprise to the team at York University, in Toronto, who set out to identify whether the relationship between the number of calories consumed, the amount of physical exercise, and the intake of macronutrients (protein, fat, carbohydrates) has changed over time in regard to obesity. They discovered that when all three factors were equal, an individual, in 2006, would have a body mass index of about 2.3 points greater (or about 10 percent higher) than a person in 1988. This is definitely not great news for people of today, especially those who are struggling to maintain a healthy weight.

According to Professor Jennifer Kuk, in the School of Kinesiology and Health Science study, their findings suggest that "if you are 40 years old now, you'd have to eat less and exercise much more than if you were a 40-year-old in 1971, to prevent gaining weight. However, food and exercise are not the only players in this scene; there are specific changes contributing to the rise in obesity, beyond just diet and exercise."

The Underlying Causes of Obesity

1. Chemical exposure

Pesticides, and some of the chemicals in plastics, food packaging, health and beauty products, furniture, and other everyday products, may contribute to weight gain. This is mainly associated with their ability to disrupt hormone function and balance.

2. Altered gut environment

Today, people are consuming more meat than they did two to three decades ago, and most animal products harbor antibiotics, steroids, and hormones, which affect the altered gut environment. So, the population of microorganisms in the gut, or the microbiome, is not same as it used to be in the 1980s. It's known that certain bacteria living in the gut have an impact on weight gain and obesity.

3. Artificial sweeteners

The popularity of artificial sweeteners can make you fat. People have a love affair with consuming refined, processed foods. They love it, which has been shown to have a detrimental impact on beneficial bacteria in the gut.

4. Prescription antidepressant use

A report from the Center for Disease Control and Prevention's National Center for Health Statistics, in 2011, stated that the rate of antidepressant use in the United States increased nearly 400%, since 1988. It pointed out that about 11% of Americans, aged 12 or older, take these medications. Antidepressants have been found to have a highly undesirable side effect: weight gain. Experts report that up to 25% of people who take antidepressants can expect to pack on an extra 10 pounds or more.

Life expectancy is going down, and weight and obesity are the main reasons, because of the food and medication industry.

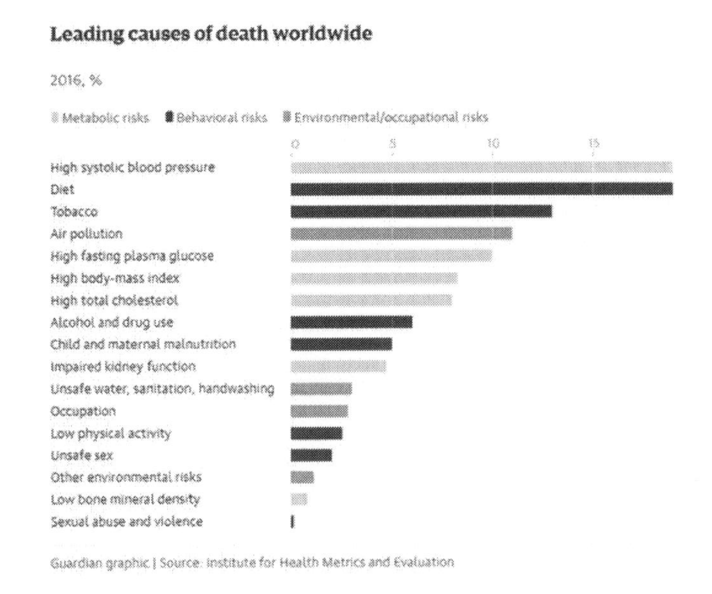

The World Health Organization (WHO) revealed data stating that in the last 30 years, obesity rates have doubled in adults, tripled in children, and quadrupled in adolescents, which means, with time, health gets worse. Solving such problems is so complicated that the faster we start, and the younger, the easier we can solve this problem. It could take time to deal with such a global problem, but we need to at least start. It is better than being killed by our own hands, and killing our children too.

Poor diet is a factor in one in five deaths around the world, according to the most comprehensive study ever carried out on the subject.

Millions of people are eating the wrong sorts of food, aiming to achieve good health. They are not aware of what damage they are causing themselves by eating such food, which they think is good for them. Eating a diet that is low in whole grains, with not enough fruit, nuts, and seeds, or fish oils, but is sadly high in salt, sugar, and fat, is raising the risk of early death, according to the huge and ongoing study by the Global Burden of Disease.

The study, based at the Institute of Health Metrics and Evaluation, at the University of Washington, compiles data from every country in the world, and makes informed estimates where there are gaps.

Diet is the second highest risk factor for early death, after smoking. The high risks of high blood glucose can lead to diabetes, high blood pressure, high body mass index (BMI), which is a measure of obesity, and high total cholesterol. All of these can be related to eating the wrong foods, and far too little, or none, of the good food, although there are also other causes.

Professor John Newton, director of health improvement at Public Health England, said the studies show how quickly diet and obesity-related disease is spreading around the world. "I don't think people realise how quickly the focus is shifting toward non-communicable disease (such as cancer, heart disease, and stroke), and diseases that come with development, in particular, related to poor diet. The numbers are quite shocking in my view."

No country in the world has been able to solve the problem of the food-related diseases, which we really need to think about tackling globally.

Today, 72% of deaths are from non-communicable diseases for which obesity and diet are among the risk factors, with ischaemic heart disease as the leading cause worldwide of early deaths, including in the UK. Lung cancer, stroke, lung disease (chronic obstructive pulmonary disorder), and Alzheimer's are the other main causes in the UK.

In general, obesity is one of the major reasons that over a billion people worldwide are living with mental health and substance misuse disorder.

If you wait until you have developed one of these conditions, before thinking about your wider health, you will already have reduced your life expectancy.

Food Industry Is Out for Its Profit Only

One of the biggest problems of the 21st century is that the food industry is out for its own profit, and has no interest in our health. Food manufacturers put sugar in everything, ignoring all the evidence of the harmful effect on our nervous system and our lives. It makes their food taste better, and makes you want to eat more. As they add refined sugar, which makes you feel satisfied for a short time, but then it drops your blood sugar quickly, it drives you to eat more and spend extra money to increase their profit.

Restaurants have thousands of secret dealings with fast food. They want customers to have these hits of sugar, salt, and fat, which makes everyone love them. An example is when restaurants give you an unlimited amount of bread at the beginning of the meal. They do not do it to fill you up but for their own financial benefits for themselves. White bread turns into sugar almost immediately, because it is all processed, and when it changes to sugar, it gives the body a craving for more sugar—so you order more and eat more.

Suggestions to Combat the Global Diet Problem

As far as most food-related disease studies show, there is an increase in the level and the size of diet-related disease problems, on a global scale. The following suggestions need to be done urgently, on a global level, to hopefully solve and control the disease and death related to food.

1. We are in a tipping point moment, and we need to start a food revolution as soon as possible—a war against food factories and food marketing—to stop them from killing us, and our families, in silence.

2. Stop all the advertisements that promote all the sugary, fatty, and salty foods.

3. We must solve the labelling problems. Sadly, this is a massive problem. Labelling is an absolute farce and has got to be changed. The labelling is a disgrace. For example, it is well known that fat, sugar, and salt are harmful to all of us, and by adding them to the food, it makes it taste better and makes us like it, despite most of us being aware that it puts us at a huge health risk. They might write that a food is low in fat, but they do not tell you that they reduced the fat but added a massive amount of sugar and/or salt.

\4. It should be clear and easy to read. All the unhealthy ingredients must be listed on the label, in clear, bold font.

5. They must maximize the small, unreadable toxic and harmful ingredients, so that it is clear to the consumers what the product includes, and how much they put the consumer at risk from consuming such products. Presently, they write any unhealthy ingredient, which they must include on the label, in very small writing, so that you hardly see it.

   I believe there is a conspiracy amongst all of the food manufacturing companies. They do not seem to have any ethics, and it is quite shocking and scary. You see products that say they are fat reduced, and you think that must be healthy. Well, the reality is, if they reduce the fat, they take away the flavour, so the only way they can add the flavour back in is by adding sugar. So, reducing the fat means they've doubled the sugar, and if they say the sugar is reduced, it's because they've doubled the fat or salt. So, it's all a trick, as some products could include far more than the recommended daily allowances of sugar, fat, or salt.

6. Use the power of social media and the TV, by adding programs to increase food awareness.

7. Call for the world population to suggest going back to plant food. Involving the nation is the best way to make them take responsibility and change themselves by committing to do their best.

8. It is a global problem, so each country must have their sleeves up and put a bigger effort into producing the largest amount of sufficient plant food. Each plant grows better in their soil. For example, acacia fibre, which grows in Senegal, Somalia, and Sudan only, is used for 90% of the world's medication, and it is full of good nutrition. If each country would do the best to grow what their country's soil can give, all the world can benefit.

9. Start food education at the toddler age, and continue through high school and even university:

   Introduce soft toys in the shape of fruits, vegetables, and seeds, with food scents when it is possible.

   Provide games and programs for young children, using the 5 senses to explain when it is healthy and unhealthy to eat each food. We need to increase moderated food education for children and parents.

   Create cartons of real food (vegetables, fruits, and seeds), and have plays with characters aiming to provide more food education and to bring the attention to the unfamiliar advantages and disadvantages of each food. For example, the benefit of banana skin, as well as how some seeds are more beneficial than the parts we actually eat. Good characters are good foods, like seeds, vegetables, and fruits, but bad foods are the enemies, like the processed, sugary, and fatty foods.

All the schools and the activities leaders must replace chocolate and candy, with vegetables and fruits, and not allow these to be sold in the school cafeteria.

There should be new scales to monitor all the schools' meals: millions of children eat twice a day (up to180 days a year) at the school, and most schools are limiting the food budget. Each child should have at least 5 different fruits and vegetables a day, instead of being provided with fast food, which is highly processed, with massive amounts of additives.

Educational and treatment plans need to be shared between education, health authorities, and armed forces, to provide intensive free training and education, for the students and the teachers at the same time, who wish to move from an unhealthy lifestyle to a better, healthy one. Since they spend 8 hours a day in the school together, they can join the same treatment plan during the school hours.

Food education needs to be part of compulsory education, and there should be no GCSE, or A level Pass, without passing this healthy lifestyle training. Each student must be able to cook at least 20 healthy foods.

10. Offer free, healthy ingredient replacements, at all big, small, or fast food restaurants, and provide them with plans to change their food business from harmful to healthy, without losing much profit.

11. Finally, I agree with Jamie Oliver that the world's governments have to organize a project of at least 10 years, where we need to get the go-ahead to work with all the fast food providers and the restaurant industries, within 5–7 years, to wean us off the extreme amounts of fat, sugar, and all other non-food ingredients.

Now, come with me to the best food and drink to nourish your body and soul. You will be extremely surprised at the meditation effect site to side with feeding too.

Chapter 5

Healing Yourself via Water and Fluid

How Much Water Does Your Body Need?

About 60-72% of human weight—not including fat—is water (reducing to about 56% in older men, and 47% in older women). There is around 45 liters in a 70kg man, and a little less in a woman. Most of this is contained in our body cells. The rest is part of the fluid that surrounds cells and plasma.

How Do Our Bodies Lose Water?

It could be interesting and helpful for you to understand and know how we lose fluid from our body, and why you need to keep your body hydrated 24/7.

You lose up to 50% of your body fluid via your urine, along with the toxins from your food and drink after it is digested, as well as from any medication you are consuming. So, if you are under treatment, try to drink more fluid in order to evacuate the rest of the medication, after you get the benefit of it, and before you get any damage as a result of toxic side effects.

You need to be aware that you lose important minerals, like calcium, potassium, and sodium, which your body needs to maintain fluid balance, so you must drink enough water to replace the lost fluids and electrolytes; otherwise, you will become dehydrated.

The Risk of Dehydration and Its Relationship with Illness

There is no life without water. There are so many reasons for dehydration: not drinking enough fluid to replace what we lose, climate, physical activities, diet, illness (persistent vomiting and diarrhea), or sweating from a fever.

Whatever the reason for the dehydration, it is serious and sometimes life-threatening. Dehydration lowers the blood volume and then drops the blood pressure. The amount of oxygen in your body also drops, which has a huge, negative impact on all the organs' functioning. For example, as a result of dehydration, your brain becomes unable to perform its normal functions, including attention and memory. The sodium and electrolyte levels in the body become concentrated, which causes many cognitive changes.

The blood that is circulating slows down, causing many problems, including a faster heartbeat, which can cause you to feel palpitations and dizziness.

The urine becomes highly concentrated due to activation of vasopressin, which occurs as a result of an increase in serum osmolality. Dehydration puts the kidneys at high risk. It also increases muscular, back, and joint pain. The spinal column is made up of 24 separate bones to protect the spinal cord, and there are discs in between each of the vertebrae. These intervertebral discs can be described as soft, jelly-like substances in the body, and they're composed of water. These discs act as a cushion for the spine, and they make movements much smoother and more comfortable. When you're dehydrated, these discs are not cushioning your movements as they should be—they become harder, causing you pain.

All of us are at risk of dehydration, but babies and children are at higher risk, as they have a low body weight and are sensitive to even small amounts of fluid loss. They might be so busy discovering the world that they need to be reminded to drink. People with long-term health conditions, such as diabetes, heart disease, and cancer, are also at higher risk for dehydration, as well as pregnant women. Elderly people also have to be careful, because aging decreases the sense of being thirsty, which leads to a reduced fluid consumption, so they become more susceptible to dehydration from losing even a small amount of body water. It could also be related to disease-related factors, such as incontinence, which can increase water loss.

The Disadvantage of Drinking While Standing

1. Drinking water while standing can cause arthritis, which is one of the problems that could affect you at a later age. Drinking while standing disrupts the balance of the fluids in your body, and it causes you a greater

accumulation of fluid in the joints, thus triggering arthritis.

2. When you are drinking while standing, the water splashes in your stomach, and it can be much worse if you drink water fast while in a standing position. It forces the fluid to flow to your gut while splashing on the stomach wall, causing long-term damage to your digestive system by harming the stomach wall and the gastrointestinal tract.

3. It does not satisfy your thirst, so you will still feel thirsty.

4. Drinking while standing increases the possibility of suffering from indigestion problem, but drinking while sitting relaxes and eases your digesting, because your nervous system and muscles are in the relax response.

5. It will be harder for the kidneys: It doesn't help the filtration process of water, by the kidneys, but impurities remain in the kidneys and bladder, which can lead to urinary tract infection and permanent kidney damage.

6. Water must be consumed in slow, small swigs, while sitting down. This helps to properly dilute the acid levels in the body by getting combined with the necessary proportion of water.

7. It causes ulcers and heartburn, as it causes the stomach

acid to flow and hit the esophagus.

8. Drinking while standing activates the state of a fight and flight system, which causes nervous tension in the body, but when you sit down and sip water, a parasympathetic system, also referred to as the rest and digest system, comes into the fray, which helps to calm your senses and ease the process of digestion.

Our toxic lifestyle made our body acidic, exerts stat that subtle changes in the PH of the body's inner environment can affect the overt health via alkaline life water which hardly to get it except from some mountains, but the Japanese managed to develop a water Machine called Kangan - which means back to life which allows you to have daily a life water straight from your tap water.

Detoxify Your Body with Juices and Teas

You need to replace your unhealthy drinks with healthy fruit and vegetable juices and teas, especially those that are rich in vitamin C, as they have an effect on promoting the regeneration of new tissues. They have the function of diuresis, which helps increase the urine volume and remove more wastes from your body. Drinking and eating the following will help to purify your blood:

1. Cranberry juice: Cranberry juice is considered to be a super juice. It is rich in proanthocyanidins, which help

to prevent bacteria from sticking to the walls of the uterus and bladder. One glass of cranberry juice can prevent urinary tract infection, as it is rich in natural antibiotics.

2. Lime juice: Lime juice detoxifies the body and gets rid of free radicals and uric acid. It has an acidic nature that helps break down food and aids in smoother digestion, so it improves appetite and eases constipation, which allows the absorption of enough nutrition from food. Lime juice also keeps blood glucose stable: According to the American Diabetes Association, limes are considered as a diabetes super food, because the high dietary fibre can regulate the body's absorption of sugar into the bloodstream, reducing the occurrence of blood sugar spikes. Lime is rich in vitamin C content, which is a great antioxidant, and is far higher in vitamin C than the rest of the citrus fruits.

3. Wheatgrass juice: Wheatgrass reduces hypertension through dilating the blood pathways all over the body, and strengthens the function of all the organs.

   Warning: If your potassium level is higher than the normal level, wheatgrass must be avoided.

4. Nettle leaf tea: Nettle tea can lower high Creatinine levels in the blood, and improve kidney functions, by removing waste products via elimination, removing

excessive uric acid from the blood, increasing urine production, and removing excessive wastes, toxins, and extra water from the body. It is anti-inflammatory, so it soothes inflammation and helps dissolve kidney stones.

5. Dandelion root tea: Since ancient times, people have used dandelion root to treat a number of different health conditions, and it is heralded as one of the safest herbal remedies available to treat kidney disease. As a natural herb, it has important medical value. Dandelion root tea can be regarded as a natural diuretic, and the seeds and flowers remove toxins from the blood and evacuate it away from the body naturally, to treat infections. It also soothes inflammation and helps dissolve kidney stones.

7. Lemon ginger tea: This tea detoxifies your body and eliminates toxins. It relieves stress and helps with mood swings, and it fights flus, coughs, and colds. It also aids in digestion, eases joint pain in arthritis, improves immunity, enhances blood flow, prevents heart disease, cures low-grade fever, and refreshes the mind. It's an anti-inflammatory, detoxifying the blood and reducing the risk of developing urinary tract infection.

8. Pomegranate juice: Pomegranate is a popular fruit and is rich in nutrients. It helps prevent cardiovascular disease and high blood pressure, and it works as a blood thinner to help lower LDL cholesterol levels and

increase blood vessel elasticity. It alleviates anaemia, enhances the immune system, and eliminate toxins as it is rich in fibre, which is good for the digestive system. Pomegranate is alkaloid and is anti-infective.

Warning: Pomegranate contains rich phosphorus and potassium, so kidney patients need to take care not to overdrink it, especially if their blood tests show any abnormality.

9. Aloe vera juice: This juice is known to support treating respiratory diseases, breathing difficulties, flus, bronchitis, herpes, stuffy noses, and other respiratory disorders. It is a great source of vitamins A, B1, B6, B12, C, and E, as well as folic acid and niacin. It boosts the immune system and remove wastes and toxins from the body. Aloe Vera is also rich in minerals, like copper, iron, sodium, and calcium.

   Warning: If your blood tests are normal, drinking a glass of aloe vera, daily, is good for you, but if your potassium is high, you must avoid it and drink another healthy drink from this list.

10. Carrot juice: Carrot juice is rich in vitamins A, B, C, and B2, as well as in protein, iron, sugar, and fibre. It reduce the risks of various cancers, improves eyesight, and lowers high blood pressure, blood cholesterol, and creatinine levels, along with increasing blood flow and

boosting the immune system.

Warning: It should be limited if your blood tests show that your potassium level is high.

The Plant Milk Alternative to Animal Milk

Humans are the only ones from the animal kingdom that drink milk other than from breast feeding, so they suffer from osteoporosis. There is so much evidence suggesting that the early faith in milk was misplaced, and has been building up for decades.

For those who can't stop drinking milk, or use milk in their cooking, I suggest soya milk, almond milk, rice milk, coconut milk, hemp milk, or cashew milk as an alternative to animal milk, which has a very negative impact on our general health.

The Negative Effect of Animal Milk, and Especially Cow's Milk:

1. Cow's milk lacks the proper amounts of iron, vitamin C, and other nutrients that we need, especially for infants. It may even cause iron-deficiency in some babies.

2. Cow's milk protein irritates the lining of the stomach and intestines, and sometimes leads to a loss of blood into the stools.

3. Cow's milk is a foreign substance that has pervaded every corner of our diets, starting with artificial infant feedings, which causes so many health problems. While there are literally thousands of research studies, each revealing at least one of milk's hazards, people need to go to the real research and learn the truth for themselves. They should be very suspicious of these foreign foods being pushed on their children and themselves.

4. Some of the dangers of cow's milk consumption relates more to adults than to children. Parents' actions form the basis for lifelong dairy-consuming habits in their children.

5. The proteins in cow's milk are different from a human mother's milk proteins, and they cause problems with digestion, intolerance, impaired absorption of other nutrients, and autoimmune reactions. Few of the proteins meant for baby cows are found naturally in a human mother's milk, and none are found in any natural adult human food. Even the high protein content in cow's milk creates problems. Cows receive lots of hormones, which are harmful for humans in the long term, and children and adults are not meant to consume hormones. Cows have been selectively bred over time to create high levels of these hormones—those being the cows that grow the fastest and produce the greatest amount of milk.

Cows also concentrate pesticides and pollutants into their milk fat, from their high dietary food and water requirements. The high amount of drugs now given to cows adds to this chemical soup.

6. Heavy milk consumption is associated with increased osteoporosis. Decades of effort to demonstrate that high calcium diets, chiefly derived from dairy products, build strong bones, have failed to prove any such correlation. In fact, the opposite seems to be true. It appears that high calcium intake before puberty, and especially in young childhood, may have some slight positive effect on bones, but this diet is not the answer. A balanced intake of all the bone minerals, along with adequate vitamin A, C, D & K, is what is truly needed.

A balanced intake of minerals cannot occur when the diet emphasizes dairy. Dairy's high calcium causes relative deficiencies in magnesium and other bone-building minerals, and its high phosphorus and animal protein reduces calcium availability.

Let's find out the safer, healthier food that can support a growing and healthy family, and have an outstanding healing effect on the damage done by the harmful, damaging food.

Chapter 6

The Real Healthy Food for Healing

Vegetables as Food and for Healing

Vegetables are an important part of healthy eating, and they provide a source of many nutrients, including potassium, fiber, folate (folic acid), and vitamins. In this chapter, you will be surprised at the amount of vegetables that can be used to heal you from so many problems, especially if you listen to your body early, and eat in moderation.

1. Asparagus: Asparagus is rich in vitamins A, C, and K, and folic acid, has essential nutrients to protect our eyes, skin, and immune system.

2. Broccoli: Broccoli is an edible green plant from the cabbage family, and it is rich in vitamin K and C. Broccoli soup can help clear your body by increasing the output of wastes via the urine, sweat, and bowl evacuation. Broccoli can also regulate blood pressure.

3. Cauliflower: Cauliflower is low in fat and carbohydrates but high in dietary fibre, foliate, water, and vitamin C. It strengthens the blood vessel walls, lowers high creatinine levels, protects the lining of your stomach, and improves your immune system. It is anti-oxidizing, and it is an anti-inflammatory and a detoxifier. It helps with cancer prevention, and it reduces blood sugar, cholesterol, and blood pressure, along with fighting

against diabetic complications such as heart and kidney disease.

4. Beetroot: Beetroot is a magical vegetable root. It is one of the strongest antioxidants, and it cleans the blood system, improving the blood flow in the entire body and increasing the filtration of wastes and toxins. It reduces high blood pressure, and it is rich in vitamin C, magnesium, manganese, potassium, bioflavonoids, and beta-carotene. A concentrated beetroot extract, called betaine, is taken to maximize liver detoxification and prevent kidney stones.

   Warnings
   • Overconsuming beetroot may cause mild nausea, vomiting, or diarrhea.
   • Overweight people need to check with a doctor first before consuming beetroot, as it can raise cholesterol levels.
   • It is rich in potassium levels, so if you have kidney problems, diabetic, or have any health problem, you must consult your doctor for the amount of intake, based on your own condition.

5. Cabbage: Cabbage is used as a natural nourishing food. It is rich in folic acid, so it can ease anemia, boost immunity, and regulate blood sugar and blood fat. It prompts digestion and prevents constipation. It is also rich in vitamins and fiber, and can help remove waste

products and toxins from the body, and normalize blood circulation.

6. Red bell pepper: Red peppers are abundant in lycopene and antioxidants, which fight free radicals and inflammation, making the bloodstream fluent after evacuating the excessive creatinine. It is low in potassium and is an excellent source of vitamin C, A, and B6, as well as folic acid and fibre.

7. Bitter Gourd: It is not only an ingredient for cooking but is also used for medical purposes. Bitter gourd has a history as a folkloric remedy in Africa, Asia, and Latin America. It lowers high blood sugar levels, is rich in vitamin C, and prevents cardiovascular diseases. It also improves the kidney filtering rate, and is used as a treatment for immunity to prevent infections.

8. Artichoke: The artichoke has antioxidant power to prevent cancer, and it has a number of vital antioxidants and phytonutrients to fight cardiovascular disease, and to detox the liver and the digestive system. Artichokes are an excellent source of fibre and iron, and they control diabetes and improve the skin's health and appearance.

9. Lettuce: Lettuce is rich in vitamins B1, B2, B6, C, and E. It has antioxidants and beta carotene, and it contains trace elements of dietary fibre, calcium, phosphorus,

potassium, sodium, magnesium, and a small amount of copper, iron, and zinc. It improves blood circulation, and promotes the digestion and absorption of fat and protein. It protects your liver and promotes bile formation, as well as preventing cholestasis, cholelithiasis disease, and cholecystitis, and has the function of diuresis and disinfection.

10. Garlic: Garlic is a powerful, natural antibiotic. It fights the common cold, improves your immune system, lowers high cholesterol and blood pressure, eases fatigue, and prevents many diseases, such as cancer, because it contains germanium and selenium.

    Warnings and side effects of garlic

    • If you overconsume garlic, it could cause some symptoms, such as muscle aches, dizziness, heart-burn, loss of appetite, fatigue, and flatulence.

11. Jiggery: It is one of the most important but forgotten sweeteners, which can replace sugar. Jiggery is a digestive agent. In India, it is recommended to take a few grams of Jiggery after a heavy meal, especially after a meal with meat. It gives relief from constipation, and it cleans the respiratory tracts, lungs, food pipe, stomach, and intestines, and it is rich in minerals.

12. Ginger: The phenolic compounds in ginger are known to help relieve gastrointestinal (GI) irritation, stimulate

saliva and bile production, and suppress gastric contractions as food and fluids move through the GI tract. It is a home remedy for nausea, cold, and flu, and it reduces inflammation and cholesterol. It lowers the risk of blood clotting, helps to maintain healthy blood sugar, detoxifies and disinfects, and contains an aphrodisiac, so it can increase the sexual drive. Ginger helps increase blood circulation, and it has been used for years to arouse desire and enhance sexual activity.

13. Sage: Sage is known for its natural antiseptic, preservative, and bacteria killing abilities in meat.

14. Olive: Olive protects the colon, breast, and skin against cancer. It reduces pain, boosts your iron intake, and it has unsaturated fatty acids and antioxidants, so it easily breaks down and is excellent protection from stomach and gastritis ulcers. It softens the skin and slows down both the ageing of the skin and the hair graying process. It is also an anti-inflammatory and is beneficial for all kinds of liver and gallbladder problems. It lowers the level of LDL cholesterol in the blood, so it works great to lower the risk of heart disease.

15. Olive Leaf: Olive leaf was first used medicinally in Ancient Egypt, and was a symbol of heavenly power. The more recent knowledge of the olive leaf's medicinal properties dates back to the early 1800s, when pulverised leaves were used in a drink to lower fevers.

A few decades later, green olive leaves were used in tea as a treatment for malaria, and as a powerful defender against sickness. It regulates blood pressure, boosts the immune system, is an antioxidant, and protects the heart, when taken over an extended period of time.

16. Watercress: Watercress can be used as food or medically, as it can purify blood. It is rich in vitamins, minerals, protein, fibre, calcium, amino acids, and immune boosters. It is a diuretic, and it relieves skin and hair problems.

17. Black Fungus: This is a great home remedy. It lowers hypertension, and it is rich in iron and vitamins. It improves blood circulation, boosts the immune system, has antioxidant substances, is low in sodium, has anti-tumor properties, and is effective at dissolving and evacuating stones from the kidneys and urinary tract.

18. Celery: Celery is rich in minerals, and the essential oil in it soothes the nervous system. It gives stress relief, regulates the body's alkaline balance, and aids in digestion.

19. Corn: Corn is rich in vitamins and provides essential minerals.It is a whole-grain, and it lowers the risk of colon cancer, eases digestion, protects your heart, and has an anti-atherogenic effect on cholesterol levels.

Consumption of cornhusk oil lowers plasma LDL (bad) cholesterol by reducing cholesterol absorption in the body. Corn is a rich source of beta-carotene, which forms vitamin A in the body and is essential for the maintenance of good vision and skin. It controls diabetes, and corn kernels assist in the management of non-insulin dependent diabetes mellitus.

20. Turnip: Turnips are rich in vitamin C and high in fibre, and they can lower blood pressure, fight cancer, help to lose weight, and boost the immune system. They are also an anti-inflammatory.

21. Yam: Yams are a good source of manganese, copper, dietary fibre, and vitamin C and B6, which can break down a harmful substance called homocysteine to reduce the risk of heart disease and control blood pressure.

22. Cucumber: It is a supernatural diuretic vegetable that contains mostly water and is rich in antioxidants. It is helpful for detoxifying blood circulation and for preventing inflammation.

23. Eggplant: It decreases the risk of obesity, by functioning as bulking agents in the digestive system. It helps with overall mortality, diabetes, and heart disease, and promotes a healthy complexion and healthy hair. It gives you increased energy, and it is rich in fibre,

potassium, vitamin C, and vitamin B6. The phyto-nutrient content in eggplants supports heart health and reduces blood cholesterol. It's a great fighter against free radicals, and it decreases low-density lipid (LDL) levels. It is an anti-inflammatory, has anti-cancer effects, and has antioxidants that stimulate detoxifying enzymes within cells to promote cancer cell death. As a powerful antioxidant, it improves cognitive function and memory, and prevents age-related mental disorders.

24. Green Beans: They have an impressive antioxidant capacity, contain omega-3, are anti-inflammatory, and prevent type 2 diabetes.

25. White Mushrooms: They are low in calories and are rich in copper and phosphorus. Copper helps you make collagen, a protein that keeps your bones from becoming brittle. Both minerals also aid in energy production, and are rich in vitamins B-2 and B-5. They are also a good source of antioxidants.

26. Okra: Okra contains potassium, magnesium, manganese, beta carotene, Vitamins B5, B3, B1, C, and K, folic acid, and calcium. It's low in calories and has high dietary fibre. Okra has been suggested to help manage blood sugar in cases of type 1 and type 2 diabetes. It is rich in fiber, and the seeds have an antioxidant, anti-fatigue, anti-stress effect. It also lowers

cholesterol. Popular forms of okra, for medicinal purposes, include okra water, okra peels, and powdered seeds.

27. Onion: Onions are high in vitamin C. Onion and garlic contains rich phytoncides that have a strong sterilization ability, which fights against influenza virus and prevents colds. The smell of onion helps to treat insomnia, and it has a great effect on hypertension, high blood sugar, and hyperlipidemia patients. Onion is low in potassium and rich in antioxidants.

28. Green peas: Green peas are low in fat, and rich in foliate and Vitamin C, E, B1, B2, B3, and B6. They reduce homocysteine levels, which is a risk factor for heart disease, and they prevent constipation and reduce bad cholesterol. The niacin in peas helps reduce the production of triglycerides and VLDL (very low-density lipoprotein), which results in less bad cholesterol but increased HDL (good) cholesterol, and lowered triglycerides. They are also an antioxidant and anti-inflammatory, and they have zinc, Omega-3 fat, fibre, and micro-nutrients. They help to prevent stomach cancer and Alzheimer's. They're anti-aging and help to prevent wrinkles. Green peas also strengthen the immune system, and help to fight arthritis, bronchitis, osteoporosis, and candida. They boost energy, regulate blood sugar, and help to prevent heart disease.

29. Red Radish: Radishes contain vitamin C and traces of zinc, which can be helpful to strengthen immunity. They are anti-cancer: they contain a variety of enzymes that can decompose carcinogenic nitrite amine.

30. Scallion bulb (spring onion): It has a range of nutritional benefits, including healthy macronutrients and vitamins, like vitamin K. It is low in calories and fat, and rich in carbohydrates and fibre fatty acids.

31. Squash Crookneck: This has excellent amounts of vitamins A, C, E, and B6, niacin, thiamin, pantothenic acid, and folate and minerals. They are high in beta-carotene, and have anti-microbial and anti-inflammatory properties, as well as being an antioxidant.

32. Zucchini: You might be surprised to know that consuming zucchini will help you to lose weight considerably. Zucchini is extremely low in calories, but it gives you the feeling of being full. It has a high water content and is rich in fibre.

33. Turnip Greens: They are rich in vitamins, especially A, C, and K, and they are good for healthy skin and hair. They increase iron absorption, prevent osteoporosis, are very rich in calcium (providing one of the highest calcium contents per gram of any fruit or vegetable), and prevent cancer. Turnip greens and other green vegetables that contain high amounts of chlorophyll

have been shown to be effective at blocking the carcinogenic effects of heterocyclic amines. They are an excellent source of the powerful antioxidant. They also promote regularity, and maintain a healthy digestive tract. They support fertility, and help and support sleep, muscle movement, learning, and memory. They contain folate, which is also found in collard greens, and this may help with depression by preventing an excess of homocysteine from forming in the body.

34. Kale: Kale is low in calories, high in fibre, and has zero fat. It has nearly 3 grams of protein, and has vitamins A, C, and K. It also has folate (a B vitamin that's key for brain development), alpha-linolenic acid, and omega-3 fatty acid.

35. Pumpkin: It boosts immunity, is low in sodium, and is rich in minerals. It reverses skin damage and improves kidney function.

    Warning: Because pumpkin is rich in minerals, such as calcium, potassium, and phosphorus, you must be moderate with consumption. People who have high potassium and phosphorus must avoid it.

Fruit as Food and for Healing

Fruit, vegetables, and seeds are a good source of vitamins and minerals, including folate, vitamin C, and potassium. They're an excellent source of dietary fibre, which can help to maintain a healthy gut and prevent constipation and other digestion problems. A diet high in fibre can also reduce your risk of bowel cancer, and reduce the risk of many other preventable diseases, such as heart disease, high blood pressure, and cancers. The vitamins and minerals in the fruits help you feel healthy and energized. Variety and moderation, and avoiding overeating, is so important, as they can aggravate your condition. Please take into consideration your blood test results.

1. Apples: An apple a day keeps the doctor away, but what makes this fruit so special? What health benefits are associated with eating apples? As one of the most cultivated and consumed fruits in the world, apples are continually being praised as a miracle food. Apples are extremely rich in important antioxidants, flavonoids, and dietary fibre. The phytonutrients and antioxidants in apples may help reduce the risk of developing many diseases, such as cancer, hypertension, diabetes, and heart disease.

2. Jujube: Jujube is rich in protein, fat, sugar, carotene, and vitamins B, C, and P. It has some minerals: calcium, phosphorus, and iron. The jujube skin has a

tonifying effect on the spleen, and the jujube seeds can calm the mind and fight against allergies.

3. Blueberries: Blueberries are loaded with antioxidants, like anthocyanins, and vitamin A, B complex, C, and E. They contain iron and minerals, like zinc, copper, selenium, calcium, potassium, and phosphorus. They also contain protein and dietary fibre. Blueberries can boost the immune system, cleanse the blood, and support kidney function. They are rich in anthocyanins, and have anti-inflammatory properties, similar to those in aspirin.

4. Raspberries: Raspberries are high in water content, which will provide volume but not calories. Raspberries are fat free and full of fibre. Red raspberries are as good as other red and blue fruits and vegetables. They have high concentrations of anthocyanins and antioxidants, which may help lower blood pressure and improve blood vessel function.

5. Strawberries: Strawberries are rich in nutrition. They contain fructose, sucrose, citric acid, malic acid, salicylic acid, amino acid, calcium, phosphorus, iron, potassium, zinc, and chromium, as well as other essential minerals and some trace elements. They have a variety of vitamins, especially vitamin C, B1, and B2. Strawberries ease digestion, give you brighter eyes, and prevent heart disease, cancer, and scurvy.

Warning: Strawberries are not for the kidney stone patient. Strawberries are forbidden in the diet of those with kidney stones because it is rich in oxalic acid.

6. Grapefruit: It strengthens the immune system, boosts metabolism, reduces the risk of kidney stones, fights gum disease, protects against cancer, reduces stress, reduces blood pressure, lowers bad LDL cholesterol and triglycerides, and it is a good source of fiber and can be part of a healthy weight loss diet.

7. Grapes: Grapes contain powerful antioxidants and can slow or prevent many types of cancer, including esophageal, lung, and mouth cancers. They can be used to treat constipation, indigestion, and fatigue. They reduce the acidity of uric acid and eliminate acid from the body. Grape juice is one great home remedy for curing migraines.

8. Peach: Peaches are rich in minerals, such as calcium, potassium, magnesium, iron, manganese, phosphorous, zinc, and copper. Peaches are low in calories, contain no saturated fat or cholesterol, and are a good source of dietary fibre. They are a perfect snack food for losing weight.

9. Pear: Pears increase evacuation and relax the bowels. They are good for relieving constipation, and they are low in sodium but high in potassium.

10. Plum: Plums are rich in Vitamin C. They do not have saturated fats, and are full of minerals and vitamins. They support the absorption of iron into the body, which may be due to the fact that they are a good source of vitamin C.

11. Prune: Prunes contain many nutrients that can contribute to good health. Prunes are a good source of energy, and they don't cause a rapid hike in blood sugar levels. They have a mild laxative effect to relieve constipation, and to prevent the growth of colon cancer and heart disease. They reduce oxidative stress, protect the liver from many diseases, and strengthen bones.

12. Watermelon: Watermelon is rich in Vitamin A and C. It is a good diuretic, and eliminates summer heat, fever, and thirst. It reduces inflammation, relaxes the bowels, reduces the risk of forming kidney stones, and maintains your beauty. It keeps you looking young by increasing the elasticity of the skin and reducing wrinkles.

13. Coconut: Coconut is low in sodium and potassium, but it is very high in iron and vitamin B6, so it should be taken in moderation. Coconut oil improves blood cholesterol levels, and it protects against heart disease. It contains large amounts of medium chain fatty acids, which are broken down much faster than long chain

fatty acids, so they do not contribute to high cholesterol, as long chain fatty acids do.

14. Peach pulp: This is rich in protein, fat, sugar, calcium, phosphorus, iron, vitamin B, vitamin C, and water. It lowers blood pressure and is proven to be effective on extending blood vessels, and it is an anticoagulant.

15. Pineapple: Due to the high amount of vitamin C and antioxidants, pineapple supports the immune system and eye health, and it strengthens the bones. It also reduces the risk of macular degeneration, and treats inflammation and indigestion.

16. Tangerines: Tangerines are rich in vitamin C and A, and folate and potassium. Tangerines and oranges are healthy fruit choices.

17. Orange: Oranges are very rich in vitamin C. They can lower high blood pressure, improve patients' appetites, and alleviate fatigue. They help protect renal function and kill cancer cells. The nutrients in the orange can lower blood lipid; they are anti-arteriosclerosis, and help to prevent cardiovascular disease.

18. Litchi (Lychee): This fruit enhances blood formation and is a great source of magnesium, copper, iron, manganese, and folate. It is rich in potassium and antioxidants, and it prevents high blood pressure,

improves the immune system, and protects from heart disease.

19. Hawthorn: Hawthorn lowers high blood pressure and blood cholesterol, and it improves digestion, anemia, calcium deficiency, etc.

20. Guava: Guava boosts the immune system, as it is rich in vitamins. It controls blood sugar and reduces high blood pressure.

21. Fig: The fig is mentioned in the Holy Quran, along with the olive. It has high medical value because it has been used for centuries to lower high blood pressure and blood glucose. It eases and relieves constipation, and prevents and treats infections, as it is rich in anti-oxidants and is a great source of minerals, vitamins, and chlorogenic acid. It is the most nourishing of all fruits, and it is good for clearing the throat and chest, and the liver and spleen, and purifies mucus from the stomach.

22. Papaya: Papaya boosts the immune system and has anti-inflammation and anti-ageing properties. It helps keep blood pressure under control.

23. Mango: It is rich in vitamins and is known as the king of the fruit. It prevents high blood pressure, boosts the immune system, reduces digestive problems,

eliminates toxins, relieves constipation, prevents cancer, and improves sex drive and erection.

24. Rhubarb: Rhubarb provides 45% of the daily value of vitamin K. It has organic compounds, and vitamin K and B complex vitamins. It is packed with minerals, such as calcium, potassium, manganese, and magnesium, which supports healthy bone growth and can limit neuronal damage in the brain. It is even a preventative for Alzheimer's.

    Warning: Rhubarb has a high level of oxalic acid, so the leaves are toxic.

    Rhubarb can cause some side effects, such as stomach and intestinal pain, watery diarrhea, and uterine contractions. Long-term use can result in muscular weakness, bone loss, potassium loss, and irregular heart rhythm.

25. Pitaya: It is rich in protein, fibre, and vitamins B2, B3, and C, as well as in iron, water, phosphorus, magnesium, potassium, and calcium. Therefore, consuming it in a proper amount is beneficial to our health.

    Warning: The patient with renal insufficiency needs to keep a low protein diet. Pitaya contains much crude protein, which will increase the burden on the kidneys.

As a result, patients with kidney insufficiencies should limit the intake of pitaya, to avoid worsening the condition.

26. Pomelo: Pomelo is low in sodium, so it is good for heart and cerebral vascular disease patients. It reduces blood cholesterol, and it is rich in vitamins and folic acid. It helps absorb calcium, and strengthens immunity and can reduce blood sugar.

27. Amla: It is rich in Vitamin C, and has well over two dozen times more than the orange. It is also an anti-inflammatory.

28. Tomato: The tomato is rich in vitamin A and C, and has many kinds of minerals. It is low in calories, is fat-free, reduces blood pressure, eases anemia, and improves skin condition.

Warning

- Do not eat raw tomatoes on an empty stomach.
- Avoid eating green tomatoes.
- Tomatoes must be avoided with anticoagulant drugs: The tomato contains a high volume of Vitamin K, which can prompt the formation of prothrombin and coagulin, so you should avoid it when you are taking anti-coagulant drugs.
- Avoid exposing tomatoes to high heat for a long time.

29. Chestnut: The chestnut is rich in vitamins, minerals, and unsaturated fatty acids, which makes them great for preventing high blood pressure, coronary heart disease, arteriosclerosis, and osteoporosis. Riboflavin in chestnuts can relieve and treat dental ulcers. They are rich in carbohydrates and vitamin C, and can maintain the normal function of teeth, bones, and muscle.

30. Pomegranate: This fruit helps prevent cardiovascular disease and high blood pressure. It alleviates anaemia, enhances immunity, contains antioxidants, eliminates toxins, and is very rich in fibre.

    Warning: The pomegranate is rich in phosphorus and potassium, so kidney patients need to take care not to drink too much of it, and keep an eye on phosphorus and potassium levels regularly, to prevent early complications.

As a general rule, moderation and variety is so important when it comes to healthy eating and drinking. Your stomach should not receive more than 1/3 food and 1/3 drink, and you should leave the other 1/3 empty to ease your digestion.

Super Healthy Seeds

Seeds are extremely nutritious. They are great sources of fibre, and they contain hale and hearty monounsaturated and polyunsaturated fats, and many important vitamins, minerals, and antioxidants. When consumed as part of a healthy diet, seeds can help reduce blood sugar, cholesterol, and blood pressure.

1. Black Cumin Seeds: The black cumin seed (Nigella Sativa) is one of the most universally powerful medicines known to man. It is a small triangular seed from a flowering herb of the buttercup family. It is also known as the blessed seed. Black cumin has been cultivated for over two thousand years, including by the ancient Egyptians and Romans.
   The oil extracted from the seeds is particularly good for healing colds and easing a dry cough.
   Acts as a digestive tonic; eases belching
   Stimulates excretion of body wastes; expels intestinal worms
   Stimulates menstruation in women and increases the flow of breast milk for nursing mothers
   Has a positive effect on the nervous system
   Dispels fatigue and mild depression
   Beneficial for women suffering from abnormal absence of menstruation, and other menstrual difficulties
   Relieves toothache and heals gum problems

2. Flaxseeds: Flaxseeds are also known as linseeds, and they are a great source of fibre, omega-3 fats, protein, monounsaturated fat, omega-6 fats, manganese, thiamine (vitamin B1), and magnesium. Flaxseeds also contain a number of different polyphenols, especially lignans, which act as important antioxidants in the body. Lignans, as well as the fibre and omega-3 fats in flaxseeds, can all help reduce cholesterol and other risk factors for heart disease.
   Studies found that consuming flaxseeds reduced levels of bad LDL cholesterol.
   Flaxseeds help to reduce blood pressure. An analysis of 11 studies found that flax seeds could reduce blood pressure, especially when eaten daily for more than 3 months.
   Flaxseeds may shrink the growth of breast cancer. This may be due to the lignans in flaxseeds. Lignans are phytoestrogens and are similar to the female sex hormone, estrogen. Similar benefits have been shown regarding prostate cancer in men.
   Flaxseeds reduce blood sugar, which may help lower the risk of diabetes.

3. Chia Seeds: Chia seeds are very similar to flaxseeds, and they are a good source of fibre, omega-3 and omega 6 fats, protein, monounsaturated fat, thiamine, vitamin B1, magnesium, and manganese.
   Chia seeds have important antioxidant polyphenols.
   Chia seeds can increase ALA in the blood. ALA is an

important omega-3 fatty acids that can help reduce inflammation.

Your body can convert ALA into other omega-3 fats, such as eicosapentaenoic acid (EPA) and docosahexaenoic acid (DHA). This conversion process in the body is usually quite inefficient.

Whole and ground Chia seeds are able to reduce blood sugar if they are eaten immediately after the meal.

They reduce appetite, which could be your aim when you swap to the healthy foods after years of consuming unhealthy, refined foods.

They reduce risk factors of heart disease. A study of 20 people with type 2 diabetes, found that eating 37 grams of chia seeds per day, for 12 weeks, reduced blood pressure, blood sugar, and levels of several inflammatory chemicals.

4. Hemp Seeds:

   Hemp seeds are an excellent source of vegetarian protein and other essential nutrients.

   Hemp seeds are one of the few plants that are a complete protein source, because they contain essential amino acids that your body can't make.

   The protein quality of hemp seeds is better than most other plant protein sources. There is also fiber, monounsaturated fat, polyunsaturated fat, magnesium, thiamine (vitamin B1), and zinc. Omega-6 to omega-3 fats in hemp seed oil is roughly 3:1, which is considered a good ratio, and contains gamma-linolenic acid, an

important anti-inflammatory fatty acid.
Hemp seed oil has beneficial effects on heart health by increasing the amount of omega-3 fatty acids in the blood.
The anti-inflammatory action of the omega-3 fatty acids reduces the symptoms of eczema. A study found that people with eczema experienced less skin dryness and itchiness after taking hemp seed oil supplements for 20 weeks.

5. Sesame Seeds:
   Sesame seeds contain a wide nutrient profile: fibre, protein, monounsaturated fat, omega-6 fats, copper, manganese, magnesium, and a lot of lignans, particularly one called sesamin. In fact, sesame seeds are the best-known dietary source of lignans.
   Enterolactone can act as the sex hormone, estrogen, and lower-than-normal levels of this lignan in the body have been associated with heart disease and breast cancer.
   Sesame seeds improve sex hormone status for postmenopausal women.
   They significantly lower blood cholesterol.
   They reduce inflammation and oxidative stress, which can worsen symptoms of many disorders, including arthritis. A study showed that people with knee osteoarthritis had significantly fewer inflammatory chemicals in their blood after eating about 40 grams of sesame seed powder, every day, for two months.

They reduce muscle damage and oxidative stress. A study found that after eating about 40 grams of sesame seed powder per day, for 28 days, semi-professional athletes had significantly reduced muscle damage and oxidative stress, as well as increased aerobic capacity.

6. Pumpkin Seeds:
   Pumpkin seeds are one of the most commonly consumed types of seeds, and are good sources of phosphorus, monounsaturated fats, omega-6 fats, calories, fiber, protein, manganese, and magnesium. They are also a good source of phytosterols, which are plant compounds that can help lower blood cholesterol. They lower the risk of bladder stones by reducing the amount of calcium in urine.
   Pumpkin seed oil can improve symptoms of prostate and urinary disorders, reduce symptoms of overactive bladder, and improve the quality of life for men with enlarged prostates.
   Pumpkin seed oil reduces blood pressure, increases good HDL cholesterol, and improves menopause symptoms.

Oils as Food and for Healing

1. Fish oil: Fish oil is very helpful for reducing high cholesterol levels. It boosts immunity, thus protecting from inflammation and hypertension, which is usually the first symptom and biggest risk. If uncontrolled

effectively, hypertension may cause further kidney damage. Fish oil is always honoured as one of the best foods for people with hypertension, high hyperlipidemia, or high cholesterol.

2. Olive oil: It has a powerful anti-inflammatory ingredient that's comparable to over-the-counter painkillers. Olive oil contains large amounts of antioxidants, prevents strokes, and is protective against heart disease. It does not cause weight gain and obesity.

3. Safflower seed oil: This oil contains healthy fats called unsaturated fatty acids. Consuming it in moderation gives many health benefits, such as controlling blood sugar, better heart function, and lowering any inflammation in your body. People can use it topically to treat dry skin, and it is safe to use when cooking at high temperatures.

   Not all oils are safe to use for frying. Overheating delicate oils can create free radicals, but the high-oleic safflower oil is safe to cook at high temperatures.

   Safflower oil is a rich source of unsaturated fatty acids, including monounsaturated and polyunsaturated fats, which the body needs to function. Safflower oil is lower in saturated fats, (which are often considered bad fats), than olive oil, avocado oil, and sunflower oil. Safflower is also essential to regulate hormones and memory.

It is vital in allowing your body to absorb the fat-soluble vitamins, A, D, E, and K.

Warning about safflower oil:
If it is consumed in moderation, it will not cause any side effects, but as safflower can thin the blood, it may slow down the clotting of the blood, which may increase the risk of bleeding in people who have bleeding disorders, or those undergoing surgery.

4. Sacha Inchi fruit oil: The health benefits of Sacha Inca oil has only recently been discovered. It was cultivated and used as a food source, for 3,000 years, in the Amazon rainforest. The fruit that these seeds grow in is not suitable to be eaten, but when lightly roasted, with low heat, the seeds take on a crisp, nutty flavor.
   Sacha Inchi is much more than just a pleasant snack food. These seeds are rich in protein, omega 3, 6, and 9, alpha tocopherol, vitamin E, carotenoids (vitamin A), and fiber.
   This super food is easily digested and unlikely to cause allergies or irritation. The oil is also available. It has a similar flavor to olive oil, just slightly lighter and nuttier, but it contains more protein and omega 3.It's important to eat foods rich in antioxidants as well as using them topically. Two of the antioxidants found in Sacha Inchi are vitamins A and E.
   Sacha Inchi lowers LDL and raises HDL cholesterol.
   Well-being – These seeds contain a good amount of

tryptophan, a precursor for serotonin. Serotonin is a feel-good hormone and neurotransmitter that helps us deal with stress and feel calm and happy. The omega 3 also reduces inflammation in the brain, which can cause mood shifts, headaches, and more.

Weight loss – Higher serotonin levels, as it contains tryptophan, regulate appetite so we don't get cravings to overeat, or snack more than we need to.

Boosts brain health – The majority of our brain is composed of fat. We need good, healthy fats to resupply those cells and to continually fight inflammation, which could cause depression, fatigue, memory issues, and exaggerated responses to pain.

Improves circulation – Circulation is improved, while lowering blood pressure, cholesterol, and inflammation throughout the body. This makes you healthier and happier, and there is less stress on your cardiovascular system, from your arteries to your heart and beyond.

It is great for diabetic patients.

Supports bone health – Omega 3 helps the body absorb calcium. Foods rich in omega 3 improve bone density, staving off some of the deterioration that occurs as we age.

Protect sand supports vision – Vitamin E, vitamin A, and omegas in Sacha Inchi can improve vision and maintain eye health. Like the brain, the eyes rely on a good amount of fat, and are prone to inflammatory damage, especially as we get older.

Joint health – The anti-inflammatory nature of Sacha

Inchi may make it a good supplement to ease joint pain and rheumatoid arthritis. Consider combining Sacha Inchi oil with ginger, for even more benefits.
Skin and hair – Omega 3 fatty acids are vital to healthy hair and skin. They help us regulate oil production, keep skin elastic, lock in hydration, protect against sun damage, and help repair damage when it occurs.

5. Corn oil: Corn oil is a healthy edible oil that we commonly use in our cooking, like canola oil or safflower oil. Corn oil is quite healthy oil because it is composed mainly of polyunsaturated fatty acids (PUFAs), and it is and low in saturated fat. It is also used in skin and hair care.

The Benefits of Essential Oils

Essential oils have been used for thousands of years in various cultures for medicinal and health purposes. They are used for stimulating and detoxifying, and they have antibacterial, antiviral, and calming properties. Essential oils are recently gaining popularity as a natural remedy, and they don't have the massive bad side effects of certain medications. It is safe and cost-effective therapy for a number of health concerns, including depression.

Essential oils benefits are vast, and their uses range from aromatherapy, household cleaning products, personal beauty care, and natural medicine treatments.

The particles in essential oils come from distilling or extracting the different parts of plants, including the flowers, leaves, bark, roots, resin, and peels. In fact, just one drop of an essential oil can have powerful health benefits.

With the essential oils benefits, there are many ways of preventing and reversing health conditions that you could be battling for years.

1. Balance hormones – There are essential oils that can help to balance your estrogen, progesterone, cortisol, thyroid, and testosterone levels.

   Some oils, like clary sage, geranium, and thyme, help to balance out estrogen and progesterone levels in your body, which can improve conditions like infertility and PCOS, as well as PMS and menopause symptoms. An article published in Neuro Endocrinology Letters, in 2017, indicates that some essential oils, notably geranium and rose, have the ability to influence the salivary concentration of estrogen in women. This may be helpful for women who are experiencing menopausal symptoms that are caused by declining levels of estrogen secretion.

   Essential oils are also able to lower cortisol levels, which can help to improve your mood and reduce symptoms of depression. They can also increase testosterone levels, which can improve a man's libido.

2. Boost immunity and fight infections – Many essential oils have anti-inflammatory, antiviral, antibacterial, antiseptic, and anti-fungal properties that help to boost your immune system and fight infections. The chemical substances found in essential oils, such as terpenes, esters, phenolics, ethers, and ketones, have the potential to fight foreign pathogens that can threaten your health. Some of the best essential oils for your immunity include oregano, myrrh, ginger, lemon, eucalyptus, frankincense, peppermint (or Mentha piperita), and cinnamon.

   Studies have shown that essential oils effectively destroy several fungal, viral, and bacterial pathogens, including methicillin-resistant Staphylococcus aureus, Helicobacter pylori and Candida albicans infections. Because antibiotic resistance is becoming such a major threat in modern health care, using essential oils as a form of independent or combination therapy can help to fight bacterial infections in a safer and more natural way.

   Oregano oil, for instance, has powerful immune-boosting properties and has displayed both antiviral and antibacterial properties in lab studies. Oregano oil contains carvacrol and thymol, two compounds that have antimicrobial effects and can inhibit the synthesis and growth of several types of bacteria.

3. Support Digestion – Some essential oils help to relieve upset stomach, indigestion, diarrhea, stomach spasms, and even conditions of the gastrointestinal system, like IBS. Essential oils can also aid your digestion by helping to stimulate digestive enzymes that make it easier to break down and absorb the nutrients, fats, and protein that you need.

   Ginger essential oil, for example, is known to promote your digestive health by easing indigestion, constipation, and ulcers. Ginger oil stimulated gastric emptying in people with indigestion. Ginger oil is also used to relieve gas, reduce nausea, and ease abdominal pain.

   Another useful essential oil for digestion is peppermint. Peppermint oil works to provide rapid relief of IBS symptoms.

   Some other essential oils that are helpful for digestion include fennel, lemongrass, marjoram, black pepper, and juniper berry.

4. Boost energy levels – Essential oils can help to boost your energy levels, have stimulating effects, and can actually increase oxygen to your brain, which will leave you feeling refreshed, focused, and energized. Some other great essential oils for energy include grapefruit, lemon, lemongrass, eucalyptus, and rosemary.

5. Improve Brain Function – Essential oils have neuro protective effects and can help to improve cognitive performance. This is one of the most impressive essential oil benefits, and it has helped many people who are suffering from neurodegenerative diseases like Alzheimer's and dementia. Essential oils possess powerful antioxidants that work to inhibit free radical scavenging. They help to naturally improve brain function and reduce inflammation. Essential oils have also been shown to improve learning, memory, and the ability to focus. Both stimulating and sedative essential oils can be useful, as oils like peppermint can improve sustained attention over a longer period of time, while oils like lavender can be useful for people going through tough exercises or situations. Furthermore, essential oils can be useful in relieving agitation in individuals with dementia. This is due to their calming and sedative effects.

No to Animal Protein

The World Health Organization made headlines declaring processed meat to be a carcinogen, which increases your risk of colon or rectum cancer by 18%. It's not just processed meat that poses a health risk; science has known for a while that eating all kinds of animals, including white meat, is bad for you.

There are massive risks of consuming meat, so you need to be sure to eat organic, and to eat small amounts. Too much meat isn't good for your health. Choose hormone-free meat to prevent several serious long-term risks to your health. You need to think carefully about whether it is worth the risk of continuing to consume animal meat and its products.

1. Meat significantly increases your risk of cancer – Thousands of researchers have found that eating chickens, cows, and other animals promotes cancer. Studies in England and Germany showed that vegetarians were about 40 percent less likely to develop cancer, compared to meat-eaters. A Harvard study, in 2014, found that just one serving a day of red meat during adolescence was associated with a 22% higher risk of pre-menopausal, breast cancer, and that the same red meat consumption in adulthood was associated with a 13% higher risk of breast cancer overall. Meat is devoid of fiber and other nutrients that have a protective effect against cancer. Meat contains animal protein, saturated fat, and carcinogenic compounds such as heterocyclic amines (HCA) and polycyclic aromatic hydrocarbons (PAH), which are formed during the processing or cooking.

2. Meat increases your risk of heart disease and diabetes – Meat, dairy products, and eggs all contain cholesterol, and saturated fats are top killers by causing heart

attacks, strokes, diabetes, and various types of cancer. Decades of scientific study have linked dietary cholesterol to cardiovascular disease. Saturated fat is present in all meat, including fish, chicken, and turkey, even when it is cooked without the skin, and has been linked to breast cancer.

According to a study published by the American Diabetes Association, people who eat high amounts of animal protein are 22% more likely to develop diabetes, cancer, dementia, and cognitive decline. Fortunately, there are many plant-based protein sources that are low in saturated fat and won't send your LDL (bad) cholesterol levels through the roof.

3. Eating meat makes it harder to maintain a healthy body weight – Meat eaters are three times more likely than vegetarians to be obese, and nine times more likely than vegans. On average, vegans are 10 to 20 pounds lighter than adult meat eaters. Vegetarian diets are also associated with higher metabolic rates, which are around 16% faster for vegans, compared with meat eaters.

4. Meat carries the highest risk of foodborne illness – The U.S. Department of Agriculture (USDA) reports that 70% of food poisoning is caused by contaminated animal flesh. Foodborne diseases, such as E Coli, salmonella, and campylobacter can occur because

animal products are often tainted with fecal contamination during slaughter or processing. Fecal contamination in chicken, especially, is a major problem, so if you eliminate animal products from your diet, you'll also be eliminating your exposure to the most common carriers of these bacteria.

5. Meat contributes to erectile dysfunction in men – Meat, eggs, and dairy products slow the flow of blood to all the body's organs, not just the heart. It was thought that impotence was caused only by anxiety, but according to the Erectile Dysfunction Institute, up to 90% of all cases of impotence are actually physical, as opposed to psychological, meaning that the high cholesterol, obesity, diabetes, prostate cancer, inflammations, and hormonal imbalances, which eating meat causes, might also contribute to impotence. But men who do regular exercise, and eat a diet rich in flavonoids, which are found in fruits, reduce their risk of developing erectile dysfunction by over 20%. Numerous physicians and nutritionists say that the best way to prevent artery blockage, as well as multiple other conditions that cause impotence, is to eat a diet high in fiber, including plenty of fruits, vegetables, and whole grains.

6. Most meat has hormones in it – To make cows grow at an unnaturally fast rate, the cattle industry feeds them pellets full of hormones. While low levels of naturally occurring hormones are found in various foods, many

scientists are concerned that the artificial hormones injected into cows cause health problems in people who eat them. While organic or hormone-free meat might be a better option, you're also not eliminating your chances of ingesting the naturally occurring sex hormones present in the animals when they were killed. The sex hormones progesterone, testosterone, and estrogen are all naturally occurring in animals, whether they've been given artificial hormones or not, so when you eat those animals, you're also eating hormones, which has a negative effect on your health and fatality.

7. Most meats develop antibiotic resistance – Factory farms are breeding grounds for antibiotic -resistant bacteria, known as "supergerms. The antibiotics that we depend on to treat human illnesses are now used to promote growth in animals and to keep them alive in horrific living conditions that would otherwise kill them. Countless new strains of antibiotic-resistant bacteria have developed as a result. Roughly 70% of the antibiotics used in the United States each year are given to animals that are used for food. If you eat meat, you run a greater risk of making yourself antibiotic-resistant.

8. Meat increases your risk of death – As a result of all the health risks mentioned above, meat eaters just don't live as long as vegetarians and vegans. According to a study of over 70,000 people, published in the journal,

JAMA Internal Medicine, vegetarians were 12% less likely to have died during a six-year follow up period, than their meat-eating peers were.

I have presented you with a list of friendly and healthy fluids and plant foods, which can be used safely as food, and drink and are side effect free if used as a treatment for most food related diseases. In the next chapter, you will find the best and safest foods for mothers-to-be, so that they can enjoy a healthier pregnancy, and have a happy, healthy child.

Chapter 7

Pregnancy, Nutrition, and Meditation

Preparing emotionally and mentally for pregnancy, and making necessary natural feeding changes is so important for mothers and fathers-to-be. It is extremely important for a safe pregnancy and a healthy baby. Women who eat well and exercise regularly, along with getting regular prenatal care, are less likely to have complications during pregnancy.

Healthy Food and Drink During Pregnancy

During pregnancy, blood volume increases by up to 1.5 litres. Therefore, it is important to stay properly hydrated. The fetus usually gets everything it needs, but if you don't watch your water intake, you could become dehydrated. Symptoms include headache, anxiety, tiredness, bad mood, and reduced memory. If you notice any of these symptoms, you should drink clear fluids or herbal tea right away. Increasing water intake relieves constipation and reduces the risk of urinary tract infections, which are common during pregnancy. Pregnant women need at least 2.5–4 litres of water per day, but the amount you really need varies. You might need more if you are overweight.

Healthy Food, Before and During Pregnancy

Since calorie and nutrient needs are increased, it is very important that you choose nutrient-dense, healthy foods.
Maintaining a healthy diet during pregnancy is very important for you and your body. Your baby needs

additional nutrients, vitamins, and minerals. In fact, you may need 350–500 extra calories daily during the 2nd and 3rd trimesters. Low nutrients have a negative effect on your baby's development.

Poor eating habits and excess weight gain may also increase the risk of gestational diabetes and pregnancy or birth complications. It will also make it a lot harder to lose the pregnancy weight after you've given birth.

Iron: Iron is an essential mineral that is used by red blood cells as a part of hemoglobin. It is important for delivering oxygen to all cells in the body.

Pregnant women need more iron, since their blood volume is increasing. This is particularly important during the third trimester. Low levels of iron during early and mid-pregnancy may cause iron deficiency anemia, which doubles the risk of premature delivery and low birth weight. Some working women might find it hard to cover iron needs with diet alone. Eating foods that are rich in vitamin C, such as oranges or bell peppers, may also help increase the absorption of iron from meals.

Protein: During pregnancy, you need to consume extra protein and calcium to meet the needs of the growing fetus. Taking probiotic supplements during pregnancy may reduce the risk of complications, such as preeclampsia, gestational diabetes, vaginal infections, and allergies. If you decide to consume meat or chicken, get only organic, hormone-free, or free range, in small amounts. It should be boiled with vinegar and Himalayan salt, and cooked well. Organic, lean beef or chicken has high-quality animal protein.

Omega 3, 6, 9, and 12: These fatty acids are essential during pregnancy, especially the long-chain omega-3 fatty acids, DHA and EPA. These are found in high amounts in seeds (see page 55), and also in seafood, like salmon. Omega 3 helps build the brain and eyes of the fetus.

Choline: This is a strong, basic compound that is important for the synthesis and transportation of lipids in the body. Although your body makes some, you need to get choline from your diet to avoid a deficiency. It impacts liver function, healthy brain development, muscle movement, the nervous system, and metabolism. It is an essential nutrient that must be included in your diet, and it is essential for many processes in the body, including brain development. It can be found in soymilk, tofu, quinoa, broccoli, and eggs. (Be sure to get organic or free range eggs to prevent complications and health problems for you and your baby.)

A dietary survey in the US showed that over 90% of people consumed less than the recommended amount of choline. Low choline intake during pregnancy may increase the risk of neural tube defects, and possibly lead to decreased brain function.

Acacia Senegal: This reduces the complications of pregnancy, and it is associated with adverse outcomes for mother and baby, in the short and long term. The gut microbiome has been identified as a key factor for maintaining health outside of pregnancy, and could contribute to pregnancy complications. In addition, the vaginal and the recently revealed placental microbiome are altered in pregnancy, and may play a role in pregnancy complications. Probiotic supplementation could help to regulate the unbalanced microflora composition observed in obesity and diabetes. The impact of probiotics, like gum Arabic, during pregnancy and infancy, has been reviewed. There are indications for a protective role in preeclampsia, gestational diabetes mellitus, vaginal infections, maternal and infant weight gain, and allergic diseases.

Legumes: This group of food includes lentils, peas, beans, chickpeas, soybeans, and peanuts. Legumes are excellent plant-based sources of fiber, and are very rich in protein, iron, folate (B9), and calcium, all of which the body needs more of during pregnancy. Folate is one of the B-vitamins (B9). It is very important for the health of the mother and fetus, especially during the first trimester. However, some pregnant women are not consuming nearly enough folate, and this has been linked with an increased risk of neural tube defects and low birth weight. Insufficient folate intake may also cause the child to be more prone to infections and disease later in life. Legumes contain high amounts of folate. One cup of lentils, chickpeas, or black beans may provide 65–90% of the RDA (19). Furthermore, legumes are generally very high in fibre. Some varieties are also high in iron, magnesium, and potassium. Legumes are great sources of folate, fibre, and many other nutrients. Folate is a very important nutrient during pregnancy, and may reduce the risk of some birth defects and diseases.

Sweet potatoes: Sweet potatoes are very rich in beta-carotene, a plant compound that is converted into vitamin A in the body, which is essential for growth, and very important for healthy fetal development. Pregnant women are generally advised to increase their vitamin A intake by 10–40%.

Beta-carotene is a very important source of vitamin A for pregnant women. Sweet potatoes contain fibre, which may increase fullness, reduce blood sugar spikes, and improve digestive health and mobility.

Broccoli and dark, leafy greens: Broccoli and dark green vegetables, such as kale and spinach, contain many of the nutrients that pregnant women need, like fibre, vitamin C, vitamin K, vitamin A, calcium, iron, folate, and potassium. Broccoli and leafy greens are rich in antioxidants. They also contain plant compounds that benefit the immune system and digestion. Due to their high fibre content, these vegetables may also help prevent constipation. This is a very common problem among pregnant women. Consuming green, leafy vegetables has also been linked with a reduced risk of low birth weight. Broccoli and leafy greens contain most of the nutrients that pregnant women need.

Berries: Berries are packed with water, healthy carbs, fibre, antioxidants, and plant compounds. They also contain high amounts of vitamin C, which helps the body absorb iron. Vitamin C is also important for skin health and immune function. Berries have a relatively low glycemic index value, so they should not cause major spikes in blood sugar. Berries are also a great snack because they contain both water and fibre. They provide a lot of flavour and nutrition, but with relatively few calories.

Whole grains: Eating whole grains may help meet the increased calorie requirements that come with pregnancy, especially during the second and third trimesters. As opposed to refined grains, whole grains are packed with fibre, vitamins, and plant compounds. Oats and quinoa also contain a fair amount of protein, which is important during pregnancy. Additionally, whole grains are generally rich in B-vitamins, fibre, and magnesium.

Avocados: Avocados are an unusual fruit because they contain a lot of monounsaturated fatty acids, and they are high in fiber, B-vitamins (especially folate), vitamin K, potassium, copper, vitamin E, and vitamin C. Therefore, avocados are a great choice for pregnant women. The healthy fats help build the skin, brain, and tissues of the fetus, and folate may help prevent neural tube defects. Potassium may help relieve leg cramps, a side effect of pregnancy for some women. Avocados actually contain more potassium than bananas.

Fish liver oil: Fish liver oil is made from the oily liver of fish, most often cod. It is very rich in the omega-3 fatty acids, EPA and DHA, which are essential for fetal brain and eye development. Fish liver oil is also very high in vitamin D, which many people do not get enough of. It may be highly beneficial, for those who don't regularly eat seafood, to supplement with omega-3 or vitamin D.

Low vitamin D intake has been linked with an increased risk of preeclampsia. This potentially dangerous complication is characterized by high blood pressure, swelling of the hands and feet, and protein in the urine. Consuming cod liver oil during early pregnancy has been linked with higher birth weight and a lower risk of disease later in the baby's life.

Warning: it is not recommended to consume more than one serving (one tablespoon) per day, because too much preformed vitamin A can be dangerous for the fetus. High levels of omega-3 may also have blood-thinning effects.

Dried fruit: Dried fruit is generally high in calories, fibre, and various vitamins and minerals. One piece of dried fruit contains the same amount of nutrients as fresh fruit, just without all the water, and in a much smaller form. Therefore, one serving of dried fruit can provide a large percentage of the recommended intake of many vitamins and minerals, including folate, iron, and potassium.

Warning: Dried fruit also contains high amounts of natural sugar. Make sure to avoid the candied varieties, which contain even more sugar. Moderation is so important. Although dried fruit may help increase calorie and nutrient intake, it is generally not recommended to consume more than one serving at a time.

Prunes: Prunes are rich in fibre, potassium, vitamin K, and sorbitol. They are a natural laxative, and may be very helpful in relieving constipation.

Dates: Dates are high in fibre, potassium, iron, and plant compounds. Regular date consumption in the third trimester may help facilitate cervical dilation, and reduce the need to induce labour.

Gaining Weight During Pregnancy

Gaining weight during pregnancy is normal, but it is important to gain it in a healthy way. For a woman who has an average weight before pregnancy, it is okay to gain between 10–12kg during pregnancy. Overweight women should not gain more than 6–11kg. This benefits you, your baby, and your health after the pregnancy. Even though you're eating for two now, you don't need twice the calories. You actually just need about 350–500 extra calories per day, during the second and third trimesters.

The Effect of Meditation

The pregnant woman's body isn't the only key factor, but it is most important when it comes to a healthy pregnancy. The health of the pregnant woman's mind is important as well. Mindfulness meditation can support you before, during, and after pregnancy. Mindful parenting helps you and your partner to manage the stress of parenthood. The mind and body connection has a profound effect on the wellness of both mom and baby during pregnancy. Luckily, when it comes to keeping the mind healthy, you need only to have a space where you feel relaxed a few minutes a day to practice prenatal meditation. Meditation helps your baby's development, the birth outcome, and their emotional health. The mindfulness meditation can help you prevent stress, preterm birth, and to cope with the fears of childbirth. The following summarizes the most important effects of meditation:

1. Regular prenatal meditation gives you and your baby a better environment in which to grow, and it keeps the nervous system in a relaxed response. High levels of stress and anxiety increase risk factors for premature birth during pregnancy.

2. Meditation improves the body's immune function, ensuring physical wellness for mother and baby.

3. When you learn mindfulness skills as part of childbirth education, you will experience less fear about the childbirth process.

4. Meditation helps you to manage the pain of labour. One study shows that people who attended a four-day, mindfulness meditation training were able to decrease the intensity of physical pain by 40%. Pregnancy meditation tips and techniques can ease the labor process.

5. Mindfulness meditation helps you to manage the symptoms of insomnia, which helps prevent preterm birth.

6. Pregnancy meditation has a beneficial impact on your mental health, and your baby's too. It lowers the irritating stress hormone (cortisol), which has a negative impact on your baby's physical and emotional state.

7. Meditation helps you to cope with the physical and emotional changes that come with the pregnancy, and it is regulate your emotions as a result of massive changes in your life.

Risk of Chronic Disease

Lack of folic acid (Vitamin B9) could result in abnormal development of the brain and spinal cord during early pregnancy. This is preventable if the mother-to-be eats nutritional food, lives a healthy lifestyle, and avoids harmful substances.

Micronutrient status, cognition and behavioral problems in childhood: It is widely accepted that the rapid rate of growth of the brain during the last third of gestation and the early postnatal stage makes it vulnerable to an inadequate diet, although brain development continues into adulthood and micronutrient status can influence functioning beyond infancy, vitamin A plays a critical role in visual perception and a deficiency is the leading cause of childhood blindness, a lack of iodine during a critical period in brain development is associated with reduced intellectual ability, There is evidence that iron deficiency in early life adversely effect brain development, functioning is associated with the inadequate provision of vitamin B(12). The controversial suggestions that sub-clinical deficiencies of micronutrients may in industrialized societies influence anti-social behaviour and intelligence are also discussed.

The Effect of Nutrition on Your Child's IQ

When you are relaxed, happy, and get enough sleep, and when you are in love with yourself and your achievement, and you have a healthy relationship and are consuming healthy food before and during pregnancy, you have a positive impact on your child's development, which includes his IQ, and his physical and emotional state. For example, omega 3, 6, 9, and 12 promote brain health during pregnancy and early life. Omegas are crucial for brain growth and development in infants. DHA accounts for 40% of the polyunsaturated fatty acids in the brain, and 60% in the retina of the eye. Getting enough omega-3 during pregnancy has been associated with numerous benefits for the child, including:

1. Higher intelligence
2. Better communication and social skills
3. Less behavioural problems
4. Decreased risk of developmental delay
5. Numerous benefits for heart health
6. Decreased risk of ADHD, autism, and cerebral palsy

Several studies have found that children with ADHD have lower blood levels of omega-3 fatty acids, compared to their healthy peers. Consuming Omega-3 during pregnancy helps improve inattention and the ability to complete tasks, and decreases hyperactivity, impulsiveness, restlessness, and aggression.

Foods and Beverages That Must Be Avoided During Pregnancy

Pregnancy is one of the most vital and delicate times in a woman's life. Therefore, pregnant women should avoid the following harmful foods and beverages:

Fish that is high in mercury: Mercury is a highly toxic element. It is most commonly found in polluted water, and it can be toxic to the nervous system, immune system, and kidneys.

Since it is found in polluted seas, large fish that live in these oceans can accumulate high amounts of mercury. Therefore, pregnant women are advised to limit their consumption of high-mercury fish to no more than 1–2 servings per month. High-mercury fish include shark, swordfish, king mackerel, and tuna (especially albacore tuna).

Undercooked or raw fish: Raw fish, especially shellfish, can cause several infections. These include norovirus, vibrio, salmonella, listeria, and parasites.

Some of these infections only affect the mother, leaving her dehydrated and weak. Other infections may be passed on to the unborn baby, with serious, or even fatal, consequences. Pregnant women are especially susceptible to listeria infections. In fact, pregnant women are up to 20 times more likely to get infected by listeria than the general population. These bacteria can be found in soil and contaminated water or plants. Raw fish can become infected during processing, including smoking or drying. Listeria can be passed to an unborn baby through the placenta, even if the mother is not showing any signs of illness. This can lead to premature delivery, miscarriage, stillbirth, and other serious health problems. Pregnant women are therefore advised to avoid raw fish and shellfish. This includes many sushi dishes.

Undercooked, Raw, and Processed Meat: Eating undercooked or raw meat increases the risk of infection from several bacteria or parasites. These include toxoplasma, E. coli, listeria, and salmonella.

Bacteria may threaten the health of the unborn baby, possibly leading to stillbirth or severe neurological illnesses, including mental retardation, blindness, and epilepsy. Cut meat, including meat patties, burgers, and minced meat and poultry, should never be consumed raw or undercooked. Hot dogs, lunchmeat, and deli meat are also of concern. These types of meat may become infected with various bacteria during processing or storage.

Avoid processed meat: Pregnant women should not consume processed meat products unless they've been reheated until steaming hot.

Avoid raw eggs: Raw eggs can be contaminated with salmonella. Some foods that commonly contain raw eggs include lightly scrambled eggs, poached eggs, hollandaise sauce, homemade mayonnaise, salad dressings, homemade ice cream, and cake icings.

Most commercial products that contain raw eggs are made with pasteurized eggs, and are safe to consume. Pregnant women should always cook eggs thoroughly, or used pasteurized eggs.

Avoid organ meat: Organ meat is a great source of several nutrients. These include iron, vitamin B12, vitamin A, and copper, all of which are good for an expectant mother and her child.

Animal-based vitamin A: Eating animal-based vitamin A sometimes causes vitamin A toxicity, as well as abnormally high copper levels, which can result in birth defects and liver toxicity. Pregnant women should not eat organ meat more often than once a week.

Avoid caffeine: Pregnant women are generally advised to limit their caffeine intake to less than 200 mg per day, or about 2–3 cups of coffee. Caffeine is absorbed very quickly, and passes easily into the placenta and fetus. Because unborn babies and their placentas do not have the main enzyme needed to metabolize caffeine, high levels can build up, which is very risky for your child. High caffeine intake during pregnancy has been shown to restrict fetal growth and increase the risk of low birth weight at delivery. Low birth weight, defined as less than 5 lbs, 8 oz. (or 2.5 kg), is associated with an increased risk of infant death, and a higher risk of chronic diseases in adulthood, such as type 2 diabetes and heart disease.

Raw sprouts: Raw sprouts, including alfalfa, clover, radish, and mung bean sprouts, may be contaminated with salmonella. Unlike most other vegetables, these bacteria can get into the sprout seeds. They are therefore almost impossible to wash off, so pregnant women are advised to avoid raw sprouts altogether. They are safe to consume after they have been cooked well.

Unwashed fruits and vegetables: The surface of unwashed or unpeeled fruits and vegetables may be contaminated with several bacteria and parasites. These include toxoplasma, E. coli, salmonella, and listeria, which can be acquired from the soil or through handling. Contamination can actually occur at any time during production, harvest, processing, storage, transportation, or retail. Bacteria can harm both the mother and her unborn baby. One very dangerous parasite that may linger on fruits and vegetables is toxoplasma. Most infants that are infected with toxoplasma while still in the womb have no symptoms at birth. However, symptoms such as blindness or intellectual disabilities may develop later in life.

What's more, a small percentage of infected newborns have serious eye or brain damage at birth. While you're pregnant, it's very important to minimize the risk of infection by thoroughly rinsing, peeling, or cooking fruits and vegetables.

Avoid parsley: Parsley can terminate a pregnancy. It works as an abortifacient if consumed in large amounts, so it should be completely avoided during pregnancy.

Parsley oil may lead to fatal complications; it may cause severe damage to the kidneys and cause a seizure in some cases.

It contains myristicin, which may travel through your bloodstream to the placenta, and reach your baby. Myristicin can lead to increased heart rate in babies.

The presence of myristicin may lead to various other complications, such as loss of balance and dizziness.

Consumption of parsley tea may lead to an increase in myristicin and apiol, and both these components may lead to disturbing effects on your health, as well as on your baby's health.

If you consume substantial amounts of parsley oil during pregnancy, it may lead to haemoglobin issues in your baby. Apiol and myristicin can lead to uterine contractions and promote menstruation, and this may lead to miscarriage or abortion during pregnancy. It may also increase your chances of going into preterm labour.

If you are prone to allergies, then pregnancy may worsen this due to the weakened immune system.

Some women may become allergic to parsley during pregnancy and may develop rashes or other allergy symptoms.

Unpasteurized Milk, Cheese, and Fruit Juice: Raw milk and unpasteurized cheese can contain an array of harmful bacteria, including listeria, salmonella, E. coli, and campylobacter. The same goes for unpasteurized juice, which is also prone to bacterial infections. These infections can all have life-threatening consequences for an unborn baby.

Alcohol: Pregnant women are advised to completely avoid drinking alcohol, as it increases the risk of miscarriage and stillbirth. Even a small amount can negatively impact your baby's brain development. It can also cause fetal alcohol syndrome. This syndrome involves facial deformities, heart defects, and mental retardation.

Since no level of alcohol has been proven to be safe during pregnancy, it is recommended to avoid it altogether.

Processed Junk Foods: Pregnancy is a time of rapid growth. Your body needs increased amounts of many essential nutrients, including protein, folate, and iron. An optimal pregnancy diet should mainly consist of whole foods, with plenty of nutrients to fulfil the needs of the mother and growing child. Processed junk food is generally low in nutrients, and high in calories, sugar, and added fats, and it is better to be avoided completely if you wish to have a happy pregnancy and a smart, happy child. What's more, added sugar has been linked with a dramatically increased risk of developing several diseases, including type 2diabetes and heart disease. While some weight gain is necessary during pregnancy, excess weight gain has been linked to many complications and diseases. These include an increased risk of gestational diabetes or birth complications. It can also increase the risk of having an overweight child, which causes long-term health issues.

Since overweight children are much more likely to become overweight adults. Let's learn the effects of a healthy start for your children and teenagers, in the next 2 chapters.

Chapter 8

Children's Eating and Wellbeing

The Benefit of Breast Milk for the Baby and Mother

There are so many health benefits for your baby and you. The World Health Organization and UNICEF have recommended for a decade that mothers breastfeed for at least two years to build up a strong immune system for the infant, and to prevent many allergies.

Breast milk provides the ideal nutrition for infants because it lowers the baby's risk of having many health problems, such as asthma, allergies, eczema, stomach upset, diarrhea, constipation, risk of viruses, urinary tract infections, inflammatory bowel disease, gastroenteritis, ear infections, and respiratory infection.

Breastfed babies grow into more intelligent children, with IQs up to eight points higher than those who are bottle-fed. Breastfed babies are much healthier and happier than the bottle-fed child.

Breast milk is extremely nutritious food for your baby, and it enhances a baby's cognitive development, partially because it allows the baby more control in feeding. The ability to control one's own actions appears to be essential in human development.

Breastfeeding promotes a healthy, loving bond between mother and baby. The breastfed baby is always held by his/her mother for feedings, and a breastfed baby enjoys the comfort of the warm breast, and the caressing, rocking, and eye contact, before, during, and after feedings.

Breastfeeding lowers the risk of developing breast cancer later in life. When your newborn begins to suck at your breast, it release the oxytocin hormone in your body, hastening the contraction of your uterus and inducing the let-down or milk-ejection reflex, which begins your milk flow. Called the love hormone, because it is also produced during sexual intercourse and birth, oxytocin brings on a sudden feeling of contentment and pleasure as you breastfeed your baby. In this way, you and your baby become a happy team at feedings.

Bottle Feeding Problems

Today, many of the health, emotional, mental, and social problems parents have with their children are linked to new parenting and feeding techniques that have been implemented during the recent century:

Bottle-fed babies suffer from colic, which is caused by stress as a result of being regularly separated from their mothers, and the common difficulties babies have tolerating cow's milk proteins in infant formulas and breastfeeding mothers' diets.

Artificial infant feeding causes so many health problems, such as childhood diabetes, obesity, bowel disease, osteoporosis, heart disease, cataracts, ear infections, hyperactivity, and cancer. Cancer is on the rise in both children and adults, and can be strongly linked to infant feeding choices.

The proteins in cow's milk are different from the mother's milk proteins, and it causes problems of digestion, intolerance, impaired absorption of other nutrients, and autoimmune reactions. Few of the proteins meant for baby cows are found naturally in the human mother's milk. Even the high protein content in cow's milk creates problems because cows receive lots of hormones, which are harmful for humans on a long-term basis. Children and adults are not meant to consume hormones.

While one form of antioxidant, vitamin A, is added to the formula milk (but not all dairy products), it is likely counteracted by the pesticide and drug residues. The full complement of vitamin A and associated enzymes, found in vegetables and other foods, are required for cancer prevention. Most antioxidants are found in vegetables, legumes, fruits, and grains.

As I mentioned earlier, the faith in milk was misplaced and has been building up for decades. Knowing and avoiding the potentially harmful effects that the consumption of milk causes is so important. Cow's milk puts you and your children at high risk of heart disease, breast cancer, stroke, diabetes, and many other diseases because, recently, 1/2 to 2/3 of the children's diet is milk and dairy, and this leads to the insufficient intake of important vitamins, several minerals, healthy fibre, and vegetable oils. Cancer-preventing antioxidants in foods are missing in this milk diet as well.

Almost every day we have new research giving more evidence that we should eat whole grains, a serving of vegetables, two fruits per day, cashews, legumes, fish, or some other food.

Physical activity has the greatest benefit for bones. The body efficiently uses what is available to build strong bones when it senses the need. In the first 2 years, there should be milk from breast feeding, and then vegetables, seeds, fruits, oils, and complex carbohydrates, which is missing nowadays from our diet.

Toddlers' and Young Children's Diets

Children are very active and growing very quickly, no doubt! So they need a balanced diet that provides all their needs. Their brains develop rapidly, so providing the right nutrients is vital to maximise their abilities. From a young age, as soon as they start oral feeding, you need to encourage good healthy eating habits.

Babies have tiny stomachs, which means they might not be able to manage big meals, so they can have a number of nutritious snacks throughout the day. I suggest the following, in order to help your baby love healthy food:

- Mix healthy and nutritious solid food with their milk and try to introduce new food every day.

* Choose plant foods that are rich in selenium (a compound derived from various plants, such as legumes, beans, apples, peas, seeds, soya products, nuts, and most of the root vegetables (potatoes, yams, parsnips, carrots).

- Selenium is one of many vitamin and mineral resources, which is essential for brain health and physical growth. It is particularly important for pregnant women and young children to have access to these essential compounds, while the benefits of calcium are relatively well known, Selenium combines with proteins to create powerful antioxidant enzymes, which can mediate the damage done by free radicals. Selenium can also boost the immune system and facilitate healthy thyroid function.

- Sixty percent of the brain's weight is fat, so it is no wonder that deficiencies in specific kinds of fats can have huge repercussions on intelligence and behaviour.

- Your child needs 3 portions daily of seeds, fish, or organic, toxic- free meat. They should be getting a good level to help their brains develop and to boost their IQ. Seeds and nuts are very rich in essential fatty acid, but take care in case they have any allergies. You can find essential fats in flaxseed, chia seeds, pumpkin seeds, sunflower seeds, sesame seeds, and walnuts, as well as in fish, like mackerel, herring, sardines, tuna steak, and salmon.

- All food must be cooked for toddlers.

- ONLY free range chicken, free-range meat, and other non-vegetarian foods contain good quantities of easily absorbable iron, and is a protein resource.

- Whole grain foods, such as whole wheat bread, pasta, and brown rice, should be introduced gradually. It's not a good idea to feed the child whole grain foods before fruit, vegetables, and seeds; because they may fill your child up too quickly, and they won't get all the calories and nutrients they need for their brain and for development.

  Almost every day, we have new research giving more evidence that whole grains, a serving of vegetables, two fruits per day, cashews, legumes, fish, or seeds are a good enough source of protein.

- Breakfast is essential every day, as it gives children energy for busy mornings.

- Sit down and eat meals as a family, without the distractions of the television, phone, or any IT games.

- Limit snacks to fruit, seeds, and vegetables. Fruit juice or smoothies provide lots of vitamins, minerals, and fibre, which are important for fighting off illnesses and maintaining regular bowel movements.

- Children should consume at least 5–10 portions of fruit, vegetables, and seeds every day.

Foods Children Should Avoid

- All unpasteurized foods and beverages, including raw milk and unpasteurized juice and ciders
- Raw or partially cooked eggs or foods containing raw eggs
- All the non-organic meat and chicken, which might be treated with hormones or antibiotics
- Raw and undercooked meat and poultry
- Raw and undercooked fish or shellfish
- Raw sprouts
- Sugar, chocolate, and salt

It seems hard to you, but it really isn't. Always avoid taking your child out of the home hungry, and whenever you go out take homemade juice with you. Cut some vegetables and fruit, and keep them in a container for your children, because as soon as they finish their activities they will most likely be hungry and without a doubt will be happy, which makes it easy to connect them with healthy food.

Try your best while they are toddlers to introduce all the new fruits and veggies, but be careful about introducing nuts and seeds. If you have to do grocery shopping while your child is with you, and they ask for sweets, you can buy something for them, but teach them that good food must come before bad food. After your child has eaten some of the fruit, vegetables and/or the seeds that you provided them, they will not like the sweets as much, if they aren't as hungry.

The Effects of IT Games and Screens on Children's Development

Nowadays, parents and children suffer from electronic screen and video game addiction, which badly effects the children's development, health, and emotions in so many different ways.

Many of today's kids spend most of their time on electronic devices, cyber-conversing on social media, and playing video games. Some parents even provide their children with games to distract them and keep them occupied, while others believe that the IT games educate their children, but experts believe that when these distractions replace true interpersonal connections and more creative and tactile pastimes, feelings of discontent, alienation, and disconnection can result. Indeed, it is an international problem, which recently led the World Health Organization to add gaming disorder to the list of addictive mental health conditions.

There is a huge negative effect on the children's education, family relationships, social life, and personal time;

- It makes them suffer from stress, fatigue, and low concentration as adults.

- IT Games Put Children at Risk of Developing Tumours. For quite some time, there has been extensive research in the field of understanding cell phone radiation effects on children. Since they are still in a stage where their body is undergoing changes and growth, the effects of mobile radiation on them could be different from that of adults. Studies have shown a higher chance of developing non-malignant tumours, especially in the regions of the ear and the brain. The bones, tissues, and protective linings for organs, such as the brain, are still very thin in kids. Hence, it carries a potential risk of cancer.

- Disturbed Brain Activity: The brain has its own electric impulses within, which carry out communication in the neural network. In children, the waves from IT games can easily penetrate right into the interior parts of the brain, since they do not have a strong shield. After 2 minutes of using the phone for the IT games, the electrical activity inside a child's brain can be changed. This erratic activity can cause problems in mood patterns and behavioural tendencies, and they can have trouble learning new things, or focusing properly.

- Sleep Deprivation: No doubt, the screens of any electric devices are causing a crisis of sleep deprivation for all age groups.

- Obesity: Extended periods of time playing video games may possibly affect children's weight and behaviour. They might spend hours sitting, playing, and eating, and not exercising as children their age did years ago.

- Loss of Social Skills: The more your child hides behind a screen, the more socially awkward he or she becomes, and the more time a child spends using the Internet, the less healthy the parent-child relationship becomes. Thus, social incompetence and screen-time represent a bidirectional relationship.

- The Effects of IT Games on Your Child's Vision: One of the biggest health issues related to smart devices is vision related. Technology has become an integral part of our daily lives, and not only via computer games. We have become increasingly more reliant on and absorbed in technology, and many children are exposed to smart devices up to 10 hours a day. IT smart devices become an integral teaching tool in classrooms, and they are used in elementary school. School screen time, coupled with at-home smart device usage can, on average, expose a student, aged 8–18 years, to media for more than (10-14) hours a day.

For example, the frequency of myopia, also known as near-sightedness, has jumped exponentially over the last few decades. Two clear reasons for this spike in myopia are the increased amount of time spent looking at things up close, and a lack of outdoor activities. Focusing on things too close to the eyes, for a long time, puts excessive strain on the eyes.

Follow the advice below to protect your child from preventable vision damage:

- Do not allow children under 18 months of age any screen at all, except if you do a live video chat with family and friends, for no more than 10 minutes a day.

- Between the ages of 18 months to 2 years: Choose high-quality programs, and watch with them to ensure they understand what they are watching. Do not allow them more than 45–60 minutes, up to no more than 4 times a week, in order for them to have time to discover the world around them via physical activities.

- Between the ages of 2 and 5 years: Limit screen time to an hour a day. Parents should watch as well, to ensure understanding and application to their world.

- 6 years or older: Place consistent limits on the time spent, and types of media, and choose early times, as screen time affects sleep, exercise, and behaviours.

The Effect of Meditation on Their Wellbeing

Meditation can bolster children's feelings of security, empathy, and inner stability, and this, in turn, builds compassion, joy, and self-esteem. Mindfulness helps children gain self-awareness and become more confident. Children as young as age three to four can strengthen their minds and help stabilize their emotions. Young children can nourish their inner being in a gentle, holistic way.

Mindfulness is a refined process of attention that allows children to see the world through a lens of attention, balance, and compassion.

"When your child learns to look at the world with attention, balance, and compassion he/she will be able to give the world attention, balance, and compassion."

Most of today's kids exhibit elevated levels of restlessness, stress, and anxiety, but the kids who practice mindfulness tend to develop positive traits, such as increased self-control, better attentiveness during their learning, and more empathy and respect for others. In addition, meditation helps children manage to be in control when they face challenging conditions, such as stress, depression, and hyperactivity. Mindfulness can benefit them now and in the long run.

It is easy to teach your child techniques that help him/her to develop a deeper sense of self-awareness, better control of their emotions, and improved concentration, via exercises simple enough for any child to perform, such as mindful listening. Give your child gentle encouragement just as you give yourself when it comes to meditation practice. For instance, your child can be guided through a brief meditation session when he is ready to pay attention to different sounds. A regular practice of mindful listening helps children settle and relax during the learning of new challenges.

You can use the following guided meditation to bring a visual component to a very simple deep breathing exercise. You can do this standing or seated, via playing and teaching, using your body language.

- Relax your body and begin to take deep inhales and slow exhales through the nose.
- Start to take a slow, deep breath to fill your belly up with air, and ask your child to touch your belly. Bring

coloured balloons and blow them up. Expand your belly as much as you can. Your child will enjoy copying you.

- Let the air out of the balloon, and when your child understand the technique nicely, ask her to be the balloon by taking a deep breath in and then emptying the air via the nose.

- Teach your child to slowly let the air out of the balloon, at the same time (through the nose) as you release the breath from your belly.

- Let the child feel the air as it comes out, and then do it together several times in a nice relaxing way.

- Encourage your kids to feel their entire body while relaxing each time and exhaling, and at the same time, let the air release slowly from the balloon. You can even make a hissing noise to encourage them to slow down the exhale even more, while the air is being let out from the balloon. Continue for several minutes.

If the child you're teaching is younger, you can add a little more detail and fun to the exercise to keep them engaged. Young kids, especially under the age of 5, love the extra movement when they're learning to bring awareness to their breath. Encourage them to stand up in a relaxed way and follow these steps:

- Ask them to think of their favourite colour while they are relaxing, and of a happy memory and of friends.

- Teach them to be aware of their body movement during the breathing, by copying you, slowing down, and taking deep inhales through the nose, until the belly is full and the balloon is filled up.

- Ask them to stretch their feet as if they are trying to get taller to reach each side of the bed, and then touch the wall with their feet, and fill the belly with air until they feel as big as the balloon. Then have them hold their breath at the top of the inhale, and relax by letting the air out of the nose until they, and you, have no air left in the lungs.

- Ask them to do each part of the body, and bring their awareness to their breathing and their body movement.

- When you're finished guiding your child through the relaxation technique, make sure they spend at least a few minutes in quiet, and encourage them to keep their breathing slow and steady.

- Try the meditation to encourage more awareness, mindfulness, and overall balance for your kids and the whole family.

- Create relaxation games, and do the breathing exercise often with your children. It will help both of you.

Start teaching your toddler meditation via creating meditation games. Ask your child to imagine a game, a friend, or anybody he loves and likes to be with. Do your best to bring a nice memory during the breathing exercises, speak about love and connection, and help them to imagine positive commutation and relationships.

Here are a few of the benefits of children's meditation:

1. Enhance focus

   In just a generation or two, things have changed so much that our attention spans can't keep up. Between social media and technological gadgets, kids—and adults— are constantly surfing the internet, interacting via social media, and playing video games indoors instead of reading a book, taking a walk, or playing sports. Children spending long hours playing and learning at school via the screens and their devices often causes difficulties to focus and remain attentive. Meditation teaches them that it's possible to direct their attention on one thing at a time, and that it actually feels great not to be distracted.

2. Build confidence

   Mindfulness for children helps kids gain self-awareness and become more confident. The confidence develops naturally when kids learn from their meditation practice, which makes them able to face whatever challenges they have in their lives. They develop problem-solving skills, and self-respect and love.

3. Boost self-respect and self-esteem

   Due to pressures and circumstances beyond kids' control, they may sometimes feel like they're not good enough. This can be tough sometimes, especially when a child is bullied or badly teased by others. Sometimes parents might bring their own bad childhood experience to the surface of their memory, causing their children instability. The good news is that meditation can bolster children's feelings of security, empathy, and inner stability, and this, in turn, builds compassion, joy, and self-esteem. Meditation teaches kids, and adults, that right now is enough.

4. Bring happiness, and connect with others

   The more you are connected and care for the people around you, the happier you become. I discussed this in Chapter 1. We need to teach our children how to care for others. Children's meditation helps them to learn how to share their love with other children. One study in Slate Magazine, looked at the effectiveness of the Mindful Schools program on around 400 low-income, mostly minority elementary-school students. It found that after five weeks of regular mindfulness sessions, teachers reported that students became more focused, participatory, and caring. Clearly, mindful children have the tools they need to be happy children and care about others' feelings and needs.

Children grow up so quickly. In the next chapter, you will learn more about what the teenager is going through, and how to support them to live a happy, healthy life.

Chapter 9

Healthy Adolescence

Adolescence is a time of physiological and emotional upheaval. Emerging from the cocoon of childhood in a tumult of hormones, physical developments, and emotions, teenagers try to find their own place and identity. They go through lots of difficulties as a result of their parents' expectations, their family's opinions and roles, their friends, and wider peer groups and more, depending on each teenage individual. On top of homework and exams, demanding extra-curriculars, and impending decisions about their future, it is a really pressured experience, which increases stress and anxiety.

Teenagers and Family Relationships

Some parents become worried when their children move into the teenage stage. Their behaviour makes them feel that they are less important to their children. You might disagree with so many things during these years, but you need to stay calm and do your best to keep good friendships with your children. They are going through lots of stress as a result of the massive changes in their body, inside and out. Close your eyes and breathe, and remember how hard your experience was at their age. Nowadays, it is more complicated, but trust me; they will become much easier and kinder when they become more mature, sometime between now and the later stage. You could feel some negative changes in the family relationships during adolescence.

Teenagers go through lots of physical, emotional, and mental changes during the adolescence stage, and they need a lot of unconditional love, respect, and support from their parents and family, more than when they were younger, as they have lots of changes in their lives.

Avoid being angry, and do your meditation to help you cope with such changes,

When they were younger, your role was to nurture and guide them. Now you might receive lots of NOs from them: I want to wear this dress, not that; I want to play footnotes, not ice skating..., you must accept that your child is asking you for a more equal relationship, and independency, and is trying to act mature and smart, and able to make a decision for their life.

When you disagree with them, you must be patient. Accept having long discussions with them, and do not make any rash decisions or judgment. They usually improve by late adolescence as children become more mature, and you need to keep the family relationships to stay strong right through these years. Do not allow problems to flare up.

Parents and families must show their teenagers that they are there for them, and that they are the strongest and the best indefinite resource of care, love, and emotional support their needs, 24/7.

Families must give teenagers practical, financial, and material help. Most teenagers still want to spend time with their families, sharing ideas and having fun. You, as parents, need to do your meditation more often, and put your work and other problems behind you when you deal with your teenager.

Teenagers go through a lot, and it's normal to be moody or seem uncommunicative. They still need you to be closer to them, and your child loves you and wants you to be involved in her life, even though at times her attitude, behaviour, or body language might seem to say she doesn't. Maybe you need to review yourself, your sound, or your body language, or maybe you are the stopper person when it comes to your relationship with your children. So, try to find where your weakness is, and deal with it, even if you need to have expert support and advice. You need to be close to your child, not only as a parent but as a friend too, in order to protect your child from their peer influences and wrong relationships, which can cause you and your child worse stress if he/she feels stress and disrespect for their life.

Supporting them is vital to get through these challenges.

Your child needs to feel that you and your family unconditionally love him/her, and accept her/him, and give him/her the emotional support he needs with love.

You need to build and support your child's confidence, self-belief, optimism, and identity.

When your family sets rules, boundaries, and standards of behaviour, you give your child a sense of consistency and predictability.

Share with your children your life experiences and knowledge. It will be really useful to your children, even if they do not show you that they benefit from it.

Supportive and close family relationships protect your child from risky behaviour like alcohol and other drug use, and problems like depression. Your support and interest in what your child likes can boost his/her desire to do well in everything in their life. You must teach them to do what they enjoy, and at the same time, you need to direct them if they like something that could put them under any risk, or waste their time and life.

Strong family relationships can go a long way towards helping your child grow into a well-adjusted, considerate, and caring adult.

To build positive family relationships with teenagers, some daily life problems can be discussed with your children. Listen to their suggestions and advice, and no doubt you will be surprised how many problems they can solve better than you and the adult family member. We need to trust our children and believe that they are smarter than we are, but we have more knowledge and experience than they do. When you team with your teenager, all of you will be happier, and your dreams will come true.

Regular family meals: Meal times are a great chance for everyone to chat about their day, or about interesting stuff that's going on or coming up. If you encourage everyone to have a say, everybody will feel that they all have the same value, on the same level, Family time is more enjoyable and useful when the TV isn't invited, and when mobile phones and tablets are switched off and out of reach, in case somebody is attracted to them!

Family adventure and day out: A short trip or a relaxing holiday or weekend away together as a family can also build a stronger connection to each other.

Personal connection between you and your child: Inviting your child, you and her/him alone, will make you more connected and will allow you to enjoy each other's company. It can also be a chance to share thoughts and feelings. If you can, try to find opportunities for each parent to have this time with your child alone. It has a great positive impact to make your relationship stronger and healthier.

Celebrate your child's accomplishments, and share his/her disappointments: When you celebrate your child's accomplishments, and support his hobbies, it helps your child to know you're interested in him/her, and to feel that you are totally connected. They will be more relaxed and will feel safe.

Household responsibilities: Sharing household responsibilities gives children and teenagers the sense that they're making an important contribution to family life. These could be things like chores, shopping, or helping older or younger members of the family.

Family rules: Agreed-on rules, limits, and consequences give teenagers a sense of security, structure, and predictability. They help your child to know what standards apply in your family, and what will happen if she pushes the boundaries.

Family meetings: Family meetings can help to solve problems easier and quicker, with preventing any damage, and they give everyone a chance to be heard and be part of working out a solution. The most important benefit it allows teenagers to feel that he is grown up and able to prove his identity.

Your Teenager and Social Media

Many recent studies found that excessive screen time usage in adolescents is associated with the development of acute onset esotropia, or crossing of the eyes, and that limiting usage of these gadgets decreased the degree of eye crossing in these teenagers. Sometimes they need esotropia correction surgeries.

Excessive screen time can also lead to Computer Vision Syndrome, which is a combination of headaches, eyestrain, fatigue, blurry vision for distance, and excessive dry eyes. There's a number of things you can do to help avoid these symptoms:

- Check the ergonomics of the workstation: Place the screens 20 to 28 inches away from the child's eyes, and align the top of the screen at eye level so that the children look down at the screen while they work.

- Restrict entertainment-related screen time to two hours or less a day.

- Practice the 20-20-20 rule: After every 20 minutes of screen time, take a 20-second break and look 20 feet away.

- Remind children to blink regularly to avoid excessively dry eyes.

- IT And Electric Devices Cause Aches and Pains: There are increasing numbers of teenagers under the age of 16 who spend too much time looking at the IT screens. Watching TV and using mobile phones is causing increasing numbers of children and teenagers to suffer back pain. The kids who spend more time playing computer games and watching TV than doing physical activities, such as cycling, running, or climbing, have a big, negative impact on their health.

  Children and teens who experience social anxiety (feeling of discomfort or distress in social situations), or who are socially incompetent, are at particularly high risk for developing a dependence on electronic media. They prefer their activity to be surfing the Internet, video gaming, or texting and chatting via social media, more than they like to physically meet each other.

  In the past, the strong desire to belong to a social group during adolescence helped override resistance to social interaction. Nowadays, socially anxious or awkward children and teens aren't forced to practice face-to-face and eye-to-eye interaction, because some of their social needs are met online, and it is becoming harder for them to build friendships.

  It became harder to build friendships. Teens and young adults with screen-related social anxiety can be awkward or even irritating: they tend to make poor eye contact, seem distracted or not present, and are uncomfortable. Often, they seem apathetic and demonstrate passive body language, like a weak handshake. They might take a long time to answer questions, and they may be unable to engage in meaningful, reciprocal conversation. When they do open up, they may not be able to follow a conversation that takes several minutes. Because of a shortened attention span, they may not give others the sense of being heard, and they often can't seem to resonate with or mirror the other person's emotion.

- Aggression: Teenagers who play violent video games, in time, become more aggressive towards anybody around them, and the more they play violent games, the more hostile behaviour there is.

  The research team at Brock University in Canada said that their results were concerning, and they argued that violent games could reinforce the notion that aggression is an effective and appropriate way to deal with conflict and anger.

  Evidence suggests that long-term players of violent games may become more likely to react aggressively to unintentional provocations such as someone accidentally bumping into them, they added.

> The study, published in the journal, Developmental Psychology, involved 1,492 adolescents at eight high schools in Ontario,
>
> The teenager who plays violent games could "reinforce the notion that aggression is an effective and appropriate way to deal with conflict and anger," so they become more and more abrasive, and react aggressively to unintentional provocations, such as someone accidentally bumping into them,
>
> Computer games, with an aggressive character, increases the level of aggressiveness in teenagers.

Finally:

As far as the smart phones are now central to teenagers' lives and attention, we must encourage them to be engaged with mindfulness, instead of the harmful useless games. YouTube has a wealth of videos aimed at engaging teenagers with mindfulness and the cultivation of wellbeing, helping make it relevant to them.

You, as a parent, can encourage your teenager to do mindfulness, or you can visit family and child therapists who offer mindfulness for teenagers.

Even if your teenagers only grudgingly participate at first, they will thank you later. It seems safe to say that everyone who comes to mindfulness wishes they had only found it sooner.

Teenagers' and Parents' Meditation

Mindful awareness is a social-emotional learning program that helps the teenager to manage stress and anxiety, increase self-control, and sustain attention. It requires only a few minutes of mindfulness meditation practice a day. Mindful choices is an appropriate addition to any children's educational or physical activities. Meditation is also helpful for teenagers and their parents.

Mindfulness is defined as being present, aware, paying attention, seeing clearly, being openhearted, being non-judgmental, and being curious. It can decrease your stress and help you be happier. Stress has been shown to decrease your empathy and narrow your perspective, and each of these things can hinder communication with a stressed-out teen.

Explain to your teen that mindfulness can reduce their stress but also help them to achieve their goals, performance, and standardized tests.

Practicing mindfulness can help teen do better with their academic studies, because practicing meditation improves their concentration and reduces anxiety and depression.

Give attention to their talk and their interest

It is important to be non-judgmental, but you need to listen and to treat them with respect, and to encourage them to talk. Once you get the conversation going, and once you open up those channels for communication, you can take those mindfulness practices you have started and share them with your teen.

With the increase of awareness of the pressures faced by teenagers, there is the need to help guide them in dealing with the emotional realities of adolescence.

Balancing Difficulties

Most adolescence feel they are mature, and they make more food choices on their own, often in the company of influential peers.

They could escape breakfast, but then they fill themselves with fast processed food, missing lots of healthy nutrition, which they need to fuel their growth and development. Convenience foods over fresh, translates into too much fat, sodium, and sugar, and not enough of the fiber, vitamins, and minerals essential to a teen's health now and later. One of the biggest, present challenges, despite the fact that you taught them from a young age the need of eating of healthy food. Teens are aware that deciding what to eat and how much to exercise is part of growing up, but they are too busy to think about healthy eating, and they find many difficulties in balancing academic studies, sports, social activities, and whatever work they are interested in.

The Dieting Dilemma and Eating Disorders

Adolescents often feel pressured to limit what they eat, and to look as nice as they wish. They may restrict food intake to achieve a certain weight for sport.like wrestling or gymnastics, or for social events, such as proms. They might suffer from eating disorders, with symptoms like weight loss; a preoccupation with food, nutrition, or cooking; compulsive exercise; depression or social isolation; visiting the bathroom after eating; and avoiding social situations involving food.

If you suspect your child has an eating disorder, such as anorexia nervosa, bulimia, or binge eating, express your concern in a supportive manner. It's better to argue with your teen, because diagnosing and treating eating disorders is not easy and should not be ignored. Visiting a doctor, councelor, or nutritionist will show you the way out with your teenager, and you can help him via the right experience.

Healthy and Unhealthy Food for Teenagers

Here are some of the healthy foods needed for teenagers to maximise their growing, and they should prevent deadly, bad food. Teenagers must eat the following in moderation:

- Eggs: Proteins are nutrients that play the biggest role in increasing teenagers' height, so make sure that they eat free range or organic eggs, and beans, seeds, soybeans, oatmeal, organic or free-range chicken, spinach, carrots, and fruits and vegetables.

- As a teenager, you must not go without breakfast; eat a whole meal or wholegrain breakfast cereal that is low in sugar and served with plant milk, which is rich in plenty of vitamins, minerals, and fiber, or whole meal toast.

- When you go out with friends, you must carry a box of fruit or a small bag of seeds and nuts as snacks, to prevent being hungry and craving unhealthy fast food, in case you go back home late.

Help your parents by preparing lunch and dinner at home. You must, as a teenager, drink 2–3 liters of water a day, but avoid drinking half an hour before or after a meal.

Teenagers Must Avoid the Following

1. Avoid sugary drinks, like soft drinks and energy drinks. Sugar-free and acidic drinks have a negative effect on bone and dental health, and on your gut bacteria.

2. Avoid adding salt to your food.

3. Avoid eating fast food, like burgers, French fries, chips, cheese puffs, and other junk food.

4. Avoid high-fat foods.

Your body will not be able to run long on poor fuel. Compared to home-cooked food, junk food (which includes fast food) is almost always higher in fat, particularly saturated fat, and it is higher in salt and sugar, but lower in fiber, and lower in nutrients, such as calcium and iron.

Eating too much junk food can leave you feeling sluggish, but eating healthier will boost your vitality and help to keep your skin clear.

Change your meeting place. Rather than meeting up with your friends at the local takeaway shop, suggest a food outlet that serves healthier foods, such as whole meal rolls with vegetable fillings or sushi.

Do not put yourself at risk of mid-life heart attack. It may surprise you to know that you could have health problems already if you eat the above poor diet, which can cause weight gain, high blood pressure, constipation, fatigue, and concentration problems, even when you're young, and could be one of the first symptoms of very bad, preventable diseases.

Chapter 10

Elderly Meditation and Wellbeing

The Effect of Meditation on the Soul and Body of the Elderly

1. Meditation boosts memory in the elderly: The dominant long and short-term memory storage hubs both become well stimulated during meditation recall, including retrieving long lost memories. The elderly brain, through meditation, manages to retain the ability to store new memories, as well as bring old memories to life.

2. Meditation makes the organs work better: The deep breathing exercises improve circulation and blood oxygen enrichment by sending extra help to all of the organs, including the stomach, intestines, the colon, the spine, and all the joints, etc. After the meditation becomes part of their daily routine, they will notice a significant improvement in their mental and psychical state. Meditation allows an extra oxygen boost, helps the immune system, boosts lung function, and improves circulation so that the gastric, respiratory, and mobility difficulties all could be solved, and the digestive and breathing problems could be relieved.

3. Meditation stimulates the feel-good prefrontal cortex brain region: Some seniors might feel low as a result of so many changes in their lives, but they can benefit greatly from meditation because it increases the feelings of happiness in the mind. The aging senior can renew his or her zest for life.

4. Meditation helps the mind to be sharper and more able to focus, by increasing brain function. The elderly can be capable members of the family and in the community too. Meditation can make the elderly feel that they have more time to enjoy helping others, and that the senior years are more rewarding than the other life phases.

5. Meditation is the indefinite fountain of youth for both the body and brain.

Tiredness and stress can come from many sources—chronic illness, disability, or the loss of a spouse. There are many great benefits of meditation, as the stress and end-of-life worries are greatly reduced, for complete healing.

Healing the Loneliness, and Physical Activities

Going to work and being busy has a positive impact by keeping us connected and socialized with others, but when some elderly reach the later stage of life, some use it as an opportunity to enjoy what they like, which they could not do before because they were busy throughout the previous years. The Institute of Economic Affairs' surprising study shows that retirement increases the chances of suffering from clinical depression by around 40%, and of having at least one diagnosed physical illness by 60%.

The elderly might do lots of activities, which could help them to heal their loneliness and enjoy a physical, mental, and social life. By being active and doing a lot of physical activity, it helps to improve mental and physical health, both of which will help you maintain your independence as you age.

All elderly like to stay strong and independent, but some believe that since they have fewer duties, or they are worried about having an accident, they do not do exercises. The reality is that it is as important for seniors to exercise as it is for toddlers, and maybe more.

1. Prevent many diseases: The more seniors are active, the more they will be protected from many illnesses, like heart disease, diabetes, etc., as exercise improves general health It boosts the immune system, and strengthens the joints, muscles, heart and the lungs.

2. Improved mental health: The mental health benefits of exercise are nearly endless. Exercise produces endorphins (the feel good hormone), which act as a stress reliever and leaves you feeling happy and satisfied. In addition, exercise has been linked to improving sleep.

3. Decreased risk of falls: Older adults are at a higher risk of falls, which can prove to be potentially disastrous for maintaining independence. Exercise improves strength and flexibility, which also helps improve balance and coordination, reducing the risk of falls. Seniors take

much longer to recover from falls, so anything that helps avoid them in the first place is extremely important.

4. Social engagement: - Whether you join a walking group, go to group fitness classes, or visit a gardening club, exercise can be made into a fun social event. Maintaining strong social ties is important for ageing adults to feel a sense of purpose and avoid feelings of loneliness or depression. The key is to find a form of exercise you love, and it will never feel like a chore again.

5. Improved cognitive function: Regular physical activity and fine-tuned motor skills benefit cognitive function. Countless studies suggest a lower risk of dementia for physically active individuals, regardless of when you begin a routine.

Weight-bearing exercise, such as walking or jogging, can help increase the strength of bones and reduce the risk of developing osteoporosis and fractures.

Osteoporosis causes bones to become less dense and more fragile. Some people are more at risk than others. You gradually start losing bone density from around the age of 35.

Nowadays, with our unhealthy food and unhealthy lifestyle, one in two women, and one in five men, will break a bone due to osteoporosis with weight-bearing exercises, weight-bearing exercise not only do you prevent fractures, but you also can strengthen your bones and improve your general health.

The Best Brain Foods for the Elderly

Specific food products can benefit the elderly in maintaining their health and memory if they're consumed as part of a healthy lifestyle.

- Fish, such as salmon, and shellfish (crab, oysters, and scallops) boost brain function as they are rich in vitamin B12, iron, magnesium, and potassium, all of which are beneficial. They must be grilled or cooked very well.
- Berries
- Avocados
- Coffee (not more than a cup a day)
- Walnuts
- Broccoli (must be cooked well, and avoided raw)

Immune System Boosting Food to Support Wound Healing

As I explained earlier, seniors are at higher of risk of injury and illness than at other stages of their life, and they are slower healers. It is better to be safe than sorry. You do not need to wait until you are injured or have an illness to act. Have some of the following good food to support healing and boost your immune system:

- Vitamin C speeds the healing process. It is also known as ascorbic acid, which is required for the synthesis of collagen. It is also a highly effective antioxidant, protecting cells from damage by free radicals.

Eating the right foods can also greatly improve your immune function, which is necessary for speedy recovery.

- Acacia Senegal is rich with microbiome, which is very vital for regulating and boosting the immune system.

  Warning: Acacia Senegal slows the rate of absorption of some drugs, including Amoxicillin.

- Oats can strengthen the immune system and help protect against wound infection, along with the proper wound dressings to create a moist healing environment.

- Seafood, in general, is high in various nutrients for overall health, including vitamin D and selenium. Fish as shellfish are also abundant in omega-3 fatty acids, which are necessary for a multitude of bodily functions, from helping control inflammation to strengthening the immune system. Another benefit of eating fish is that it's a good source of protein, which is essential to the development of healthy new tissue.

- Barley as Oats are grains that contain beta-glucan, fiber that has strong antioxidant and antimicrobial properties. As such, they can boost immune function and, in effect, support wound healing.

- Natural unsweetened yogurt contains high levels of probiotics, a type of bacteria that's good for the digestive system and promotes immune function, which may help reduce the risk of wound infection. A plant probiotic such as Acacia Senegal is better than consuming unsweetened yogurt.

Note: You can also find a long list of food, rich in Vitamin C, in Chapter 6, The Real Healthy Food for Healing

Food for Joint and Back Health

Many elderly people could have joint and back pain, and they should not ignore it but must contact their doctor.

Eating protein-rich foods is one of the best things that you can do to help heal your wounds.

- Fish: Salmon, halibut, tuna, mackerel, sardines, and other cold-water, fish have high omega-3 fatty acid levels, making them good for the heart and brain. If seafood isn't your cup of tea, beans, nuts, flaxseeds, and healthy oils can be good substitutes.

- Fish oil: The beneficial effects of fish oils are attributed to their omega-3 fatty acid content. It has anti-inflammatory benefits and is particularly helpful for joint pain. Natural sources of fish oil include cold-water fish, such as wild salmon.

- Some vegetables and fruits: winter squash, olive oil, citrus fruit, kale, and other dark, leafy greens are rich in nutrients that are linked to joint health, including the antioxidants beta-carotene and vitamin C. Some are also an excellent source of calcium, which helps keep your bones strong.

- Berries and dark skinned fruits: They have plenty of antioxidants, which help fight damaging free radicals in the body. Blueberries, blackberries, strawberries, raspberries, plums, oranges, red grapes, and cherries are all good options.

- Beans: They are one of the most abundant sources of plant protein.

- Nuts: Like beans, nuts are an excellent source of protein.

- Carrots, spinach, sweet potatoes, and kale for vitamin A; oranges, strawberries, peppers, and broccoli for vitamin C.
- Fortified cereal
- Eggs: They must be very well boiled, or it is better to eat only the white part after being very well cooked, to prevent elevating cholesterol.
- Lean meat, lean turkey, fish, and chicken, salmon, tuna, and trout, after being very well cooked.
- If you like milk and yogurt. I recommend vegetable milk and yogurt.

Elderly people must follow their doctors' advice and treatment to speed their recovery, I recommend having at least 3–5 small servings of plant protein. Part of the protein is needed to provide your body with energy, and the rest will support healing, side by side with your prescribed treatment and to reduce the side effects of some of your medication.

Forbidden Food for Elderly People

You might be shocked to know that some healthy foods, which seem to be healthy food choices, are kinds of food that may contain bacteria, viruses, parasites, or toxins that can cause food-borne illness. They can compromise the immune function of the elderly. Seniors should avoid some foods that appear healthy, especially those served raw, because of the germs they harbor. As we age, it gets harder for our bodies to fight off infections.

They put the seniors at risk of health setbacks and complications from a bout of food poisoning. Therefore, it is crucial for seniors to be aware of what foods pose significant risks, and to make sure that they avoid them. In case they decide to eat them, they need to be cooked very, very, very well. The older we become, the weaker our immune system becomes.

- Some Raw Vegetables, like Sprouts, may contain bacteria, viruses, parasites, or toxins. Sprouts are a prime example. "Consuming broccoli sprouts, alfalfa sprouts, bean sprouts, etc. which provides a great deal of nutritional, digestive, and enzymatic benefits, but the warm, humid conditions needed to grow sprouts from seeds are also ideal for bacterial growth. Salmonella, E. coli, and other kinds of harmful bacteria can grow to high levels. When the seeds sprout, the bacteria get trapped inside, which can make us very sick."

  While sprouts are powerhouses of nutrition, which are generally harmless for healthy individuals to eat, there's no way to guarantee their safety, even with a thorough washing and proper food-handling techniques. Cooking is the only way to kill the most dangerous foodborne pathogens, which is why foods like sprouts, which are usually served raw, or at most, lightly cooked, pose the most risks to older individuals.

- Raw eggs
- Raw fish, oysters, clams and mussels
- Soft cheeses, such as Brie, Camembert, and blue-veined varieties
- Unpasteurised milk; unpasteurised juice
- Raw meat carpaccio (thin shavings of raw beef fillet), steak tartare, and dry meat.

References

The Shocking Truth About Your Health, by Lissa Rankin

https://news.harvard.edu/gazette/story/2015/10/relaxation-response-proves-positive/

http://www.unimedliving.com/living-medicine/illness-and-disease/the-roseto-effect-a-lesson-on-the-true-cause-of-heart-disease.html

https://www.bluezones.com/2018/08/moai-this-tradition-is-why-okinawan-people-live-longer-better/

https://en.wikipedia.org/wiki/Blue_Zone#/media/File:Vendiagram.gif

https://singjupost.com/lissa-rankin-the-1-public-health-issue-doctors-arent-talking-about-transcript/

https://lissarankin.com/wp-content/uploads/2012/11/tedwholehealthcairn.jpg

https://singjupost.com/is-medicine-killing-you-by-lissa-rankin-at-tedxfargo-full-transcript/2/

Mind Over Medicine, by Lissa Rankin

https://youtube/s2hLhWSIOI0

http://naturallysavvy.com/eat/3-reasons-why-were-fatter-than-30-years-ago-and-its-not-food-or-exercise/

https://www.google.com/search?ei=pTMWXPadO8LhxgOuxarwBQ&q=statastic+about+the+death+as+a+result+of+wrong+feeding&oq=statastic+about+the+death+as+a+result+of+wrong+feeding&gs_l=psy-ab.3...17248.52932..53536...16.0..0.177.6032.52j15......0....1..gws-wiz.....6..0j0i71j35i39j0i131j0i67j0i20i263j0i131i67j0i10j0i13j0i13i10j0i22i30j0i8i13i30j33i22i29i30j0i13i5i30j33i160j33i21.W-apGQJJi1E

https://www.youtube.com/results?search_query=Teach+every+child+about+food+%7C+Jamie+Oliver+Ted+ED+text+
https://www.telegraph.co.uk/news/health/news/11723443/Unhealthy-lifestyle-can-knock-23-years-off-lifespan.html

https://www.healthline.com/nutrition/13-foods-to-eat-when-pregnant#section1

https://www.ncbi.nlm.nih.gov/pubmed/20071652

https://www.ncbi.nlm.nih.gov/pubmed/18683028

https://www.ncbi.nlm.nih.gov/pubmed/19996479

https://www.ncbi.nlm.nih.gov/pubmed/22071814

https://www.healthline.com/nutrition/11-foods-to-avoid-during-pregnancy

https://news.harvard.edu/gazette/story/2015/10/relaxation-response-proves-positive/

http://www.unimedliving.com/living-medicine/illness-and-disease/the-roseto-effect-a-lesson-on-the-true-cause-of-heart-disease.html

https://www.bluezones.com/2018/08/moai-this-tradition-is-why-okinawan-people-live-longer-better/

https://en.wikipedia.org/wiki/Blue_Zone#/media/File:Vendiagram.gif

https://singjupost.com/lissa-rankin-the-1-public-health-issue-doctors-arent-talking-about-transcript/

https://lissarankin.com/wp-content/uploads/2012/11/tedwholehealthcairn.jpg

https://singjupost.com/is-medicine-killing-you-by-lissa-rankin-at-tedxfargo-full-transcript/2/

https://www.betterhealth.vic.gov.au/health/healthyliving/physical-activity-for-seniors